"This book is a microcosm of Americana during the tumultuous twentieth century. It is a striking example of how fascinating the history of the "average" American family can be. It should motivate every American to compile their own family history before the memories of their parents' and grandparents' generations are lost forever."

Nancy Sliwa, author of "Watchman, What of the Night?"

"I laughed! I cried! This book takes the reader on an incredible journey filled with insight into the lives of both Karolina and Helen. Through trials and tribulations, these women left a legacy of love and inspiration to new generations of spirited individuals. Priceless photographs, which take the reader to another time and place add to the journey. From Czechoslovakia to Arizona, the reader enjoys learning of a rich family heritage filled with countless blessings. It was a joy to read!"

Nancy Hagener, teacher/author

"Jimmie Lou Watson has captured the essence of preserving her heritage while celebrating her past. In a day where origins are seldom appreciated, "Her Spirit Lives In Us" reinvents the time-honored ceremony of honoring our ancestors. I recommend this book to anyone dealing with the loss of a loved one or searching for a way to document family origins."

Nancy Lee Hayden, owner/director, Hayden Research Center

"The tremendous history of a courageous American immigrant family from which we can all learn the spirit of integrity, faith and love. Experience the family living through the coal mines in West Virginia, big city life in Chicago, and the wild-western culture of Arizona. This book shows not just one slice of Americana, but a wide-angle view of the whole of twentieth-century living–a taste of what day-to-day life was really like."

Jamie L. Saloff, author and home-schooling mother

"This is a collection of anecdotes, but the overall impact is immense!"
John R. Hayden, designer/brother

"Really enjoyed your book—extremely interesting! This is certainly the story of the struggle and survival of so many immigrants I've known that has never been written down. They were able to live through these experiences because others were in the same boat and they helped each other."
Peter Yurich, Oak Creek, Colorado, historian

"This book is an inspiration to all of us!"
Sally Hayden Nardozzi, calligrapher/sister

"Jimmie Lou Watson's five-generation chronicle of the lives of her maternal grandmother, Karolina Grabiec, and Karolina's descendants is touching and inspirational."
Beth Phillips, Eagle Eye Editor

Her Spirit Lives In Us

Immigrant Mother's Legacy of Love

Jimmie Lou Watson

Book Ventures

Copyright © 2004

All rights reserved. No part of this work may be reproduced or transmitted in any form by any means, electronic or mechanical, including photocopying and recording, or by any information storage or retrieval system, except as may be expressly permitted by the 1976 Copyright Act or in writing by the publisher.

Unless noted New American Standard (NAS) or King James (KJ), scriptures are taken from the HOLY BIBLE, NEW INTERNATIONAL VERSION®. Copyright © 1973, 1978, 1984 by International Bible Society. Used by permission of Zondervan Publishing House. All rights reserved.

Requests for such permission should be addressed to:
Book Ventures, LLC
Phoenix, Arizona

Watson, Jimmie Lou
    Her Spirit Lives In Us: Immigrant Mother's Legacy of Love

Cover Design: Manjari Graphics
Layout: J. L. Saloff

Hardbound ISBN: 0-9762279-0-8
Perfectbound ISBN: 0-9762279-1-6
Library of Congress Control Number: 2004098254
Copyright information available upon request. v.1.01

First Edition

Printed on acid free paper in The United States of America

To Jesse, Liz, and Zac,

in loving memory of

my grandmother

Karolina

and my mother

Helen

Her Spirit Lives In Us
Immigrant Mother's Legacy of Love

Table of Contents:

"Seasons of Life" x

Preface 1

Part One: Life in the Old World

1. Karvina, Czechoslovakia 5
2. Love Story 9

Part Two: Life in West Virginia

3. New Mine—New Life 15
4. Seasons of Love 21
5. Days of Danger and Delight 27
6. The Real Survivors 35
7. Tragedies and Trials 41

Table of Contents:

Part Three: A New Beginning
8. Chicago—Starting Over 49
9. Foundations and Friends 57
10. Karolina's Spirit in Her Nine Children 63
11. West to Arizona 79
12. Karolina 91

Part Four: Legacy of Love
13. Helen's Spirit 101
14. The Power of the Home 115
15. Mom 2000-2001 133
16. Memories of Cousins and Friends 139

Part Five: Her Spirit Lives
17. Her Spirit Lives On In Us 145
18. The Fourth and Fifth Generations 155

Table of Contents:

Reflections 161

"Love Never Fails" 163

Epilogue 165

Appendix 171

Notes 173

Acknowledgements 179

Index 181

Photo Index 189

Seasons of Life

There is an appointed time for everything. And there is
a time for every event under heaven—

A time to give birth, and a time to die;
A time to plant, and a time to uproot what is planted.

A time to kill, and a time to heal;
A time to tear down, and a time to build up.

A time to weep, and a time to laugh;
A time to mourn, and a time to dance.

A time to throw stones, and a time to gather stones;
A time to embrace, and a time to shun embracing.

A time to search, and a time to give up as lost;
A time to keep, and a time to throw away.

A time to tear apart, and a time to sew together;
A time to be silent, and a time to speak.

A time to love, and a time to hate;
A time for war, and a time for peace.

What profit is there to the worker from
that in which he toils?
I have seen the task which God has given the sons of
men with which to occupy themselves.

He has made everything appropriate in its time.
He has also set eternity in their heart, yet so that
man will not find out the work which God has done from
the beginning even to the end.

I know that there is nothing better for them than
to rejoice and to do good in one's lifetime;
Moreover, that every man who eats and drinks sees
good in all his labor—it is the gift of God.

Ecclesiastes 3: 1-13 (NAS)

Preface

Musty albums, which Grandmother Karolina carefully assembled many years ago, are filled with irreplaceable and precious records of some of the events in her life. As I hold these albums, now falling apart in my hands, I treasure the old black and white photos she placed there with her own hands. She carefully glued the corners onto the pages, measuring for each photo. Many are small 1" x 1" and 2" x 2" photos.

Karolina kept her little Kodak Brownie camera handy and took hundreds of pictures in her lifetime. In Illinois she snapped loved ones on the steps of her flat and in activities at her children's homes. In Arizona she photographed activities in her yard, as well as on jaunts around Arizona with family members laughing and talking. They were happy and wanted to remember the events in their lives together. I notice that Grandmother looked happiest when photographed with family and especially with her grandchildren.

I will never forget Grandmother Karolina and her spirit of determination, faith, and love that lived on in my mother, Helen. I feel so blessed to have known these two extraordinary women, and I want to share their story. The generations who did not know them will now know how it all began—where we came from. They will know about the spirit which lived in Karolina and her children, and that it lives on in us today.

I feel happy when I think of my grandmother and mother. I remember their love and their calm, gentle manner. Even though we seem insignificant when compared to God's universe, they understood that we each have unique souls, cherished by Him.

Two events in my life triggered my writing of this book. The first was a card my cousin Linda gave me when Mom passed on into eternity. It states, "She gives us life and teaches us how to live it. Her love will always be a part of all we are. It must be hard to say good-bye to one who meant so much, but just remember that all of your mother's best qualities live on in you—yours to treasure and share through all the years to come." This card made me happy to think about the truth of these statements.

The second event was during a conversation with my son. When I said "I wasn't raised that way," he looked at me and said, "I have no idea how you were raised." I was shocked to realize that our lives had been that busy—too busy for me to have shared with my children the wonderful memories I have of my grandmother and mother.

In my research for this book I enjoyed reconnecting with my aunts and uncles, brothers and sisters, our children, cousins, nieces, nephews, and friends who knew my grandmother and/or my mother. In talking with them, I felt the warm sense of family unity—the way Karolina and Helen did. I now share what I learned from my interviews, from photos, from my memory, and from the stories Mom told me over the years.

I share the past and the present. I want to continue sharing in the future. The most important thing I can share is the spirit of love and faith my grandmother Karolina shared with us. I'm thankful that her spirit lives on in us today.

Author's Note

These events have been portrayed as I remember them and as they were told to me by family, friends, and Galloway neighbors. I took the liberty of creating the conversations of those in Czechoslovakia to catch the spirit of what may have been said over one hundred years ago.

Karolina

Part One: Life in the Old World

1

Karvina, Czechoslovakia

It is for freedom that Christ has set us free.
Galatians 5:1

Karolina Franek, my Polish grandmother, was born October 7, 1892, in Stare Mesto Frestat (now Karvina), Czechoslovakia, which is located near the Polish border in the western and more prosperous section of what is now known as the Czech Republic. Karolina's mother was Mary Marcal Franek; her father was Joseph Franek.

Karvina, Czechoslovakia

As a young woman, Karolina was one of the most beautiful women in Karvina. At the local dances people would stop and stare to admire her beauty. "She could have married any man she wanted. She could have married the richest man in Poland!" her good friend Ann Lichner alleged.

Frank Grabiec,[1] my grandfather, was born December 15, 1888,[2] to Josaphine Wrasena and Joseph Grabiec, also in Stare Mesto Frestat, Czechoslovakia (now known as Karvina in the Czech Republic). Frank also was of Polish heritage.

An accident when he was eleven affected the mind of Frank Grabiec Sr. for the rest of his life. While he was on the roof with the pigeons he raised and loved, another boy who was jealous of him tried to catch one of his pigeons. He pushed Frank, causing him to trip and fall off of the two-story building.

With his head split open Frank lay unconscious on the ground. His thirteen-year-old sister Frances was the only one home at the time. She quickly rolled him up in a *pierzyna* (unquilted feather bed) and dragged him into the house. Frank's mother, who worked as a housekeeper in Karvina, did not get home until much later. When she got home, she washed his head, pressed it together, wrapped it as tightly as she could, and waited for the doctor. She believed Frances' quick action of wrapping his head with the pierzyna saved him from bleeding to death. Young Frank was in a coma for about five weeks. He was left with a scar from the top of his head to his ear and suffered the consequences of this tragic accident for the rest of his life.

∽

Life in Czechoslovakia at this time was under the control of Austria, and schooling was not allowed for the Polish minority. So, with few other options, Frank became a coal miner. He learned mining skills in Ostrava-Karvina, the center of Czechoslovakia's main coal mining district near the Oder River.[3] For enjoyment he developed his musical talent and learned to play the violin, flute, and clarinet.

In her spirit Karolina felt that there was something more for her than life as she knew it in Karvina. She had heard about a better life in America, "the land of the free." Her brother, Rudolph, and others she knew had gone to America and had written letters about opportunities and freedoms which she could only dream about. Here in Karvina, Karolina could only do what was permitted by the Austrian government. This meant being a miner, working as a seamstress in the textile mills, or working as a governess. Karolina loved children, and, working as a governess, she enjoyed dressing up and taking the children to wonderful concerts by Ignace Paderewski, the famous Polish statesman and composer and the most beloved pianist since Franz Liszt.[4]

Thoughts of leaving the life she knew in Czechoslovakia stirred feelings of uncertainty as well as excitement and anticipation. She knew it would take courage to break away from the cycle of what was expected. Her determination compelled her, however, and she would follow her heart.

2

Love Story

In his heart a man plans his course, but the Lord determines his steps. Proverbs 16:9

She was sitting in her favorite tree at the edge of the field when he spotted her. It was a gorgeous day, full of sunshine, green hills, trees, birds—the beauty of God's creation.

"Hello!" they greeted one another. Frank stared at young Karolina. She had auburn hair—thick and long. He was struck by her beauty. She was impressed with his undaunted confidence.

Thus begins the love story that carried them across the Atlantic.

Karolina loved Frank, but he was gone. He had left for America in July 1910, at the age of twenty-one, and now worked in the coal mines of the United States. Karolina had stayed behind. She was pregnant with their first child, and she did not want to risk the trip at that time. Their daughter, Mañia, was born at the end of the year on December 31, 1910, in Karvina, Czechoslovakia. Her christening photo on the following page shows, from the left, Karolina's brother Joseph, Karolina, the midwife holding baby Mañia, Karolina's sister and her husband (names unknown).

Now it was time for Karolina to go to America. But how could she take her baby daughter? How could her baby survive such a long voyage across the Atlantic? Again, she knew she could not risk it.

1910 Mañia's Christening Day

As her baby grew, however, Karolina thought perhaps she could leave her temporarily with her mother, Mary. She could join Frank now in America, and her sister promised to bring Mañia the following year. Later Karolina could send for her mother, father, and younger brother Joseph. She had already given her older brother, Rudolph, the money he needed for his trip to America, and he was already there. Her dream was to unite the whole family in a free country with a new life and a hopeful future!

As she was planning her trip, Karolina heard about the wonderful, amazing, and *"unsinkable"* ship, the *Titanic*. Yes, this would be the safest ship to take, she thought.

"Don't go on the Titanic!" Karolina's mother warned. "I have a funny feeling about that ship...." It was 1912.

Something–a strong feeling–told Mary, Karolina's mother, there was something dangerously prophetic about calling a ship 'unsinkable.' She warned Karolina of her strong foreboding; Karolina listened and took it to heart. She would wait. Mañia was still young and needed her. But she knew Frank needed her, too. And she needed to prepare for her own future.

As the days passed, Karolina worked hard to save up for her ticket and for the rest of her family's ship fares also. But wars and rumors of wars were constantly in the air. Young men were being forced into military service—some with Germany, some with Austria; and some were still fighting for Poland, their homeland, to be free and to become a nation again. Her brother, Rudolph, had already left because he did not want to be forced into military service to possibly fight against his brother and his friends.

Karolina could not have known that World War I was looming one year away. She did know, however, that war *was* coming and knew she had to leave right then or perhaps never.

Even though news of the sinking of the *Titanic* reached the Franeks, Karolina still was determined to go. Since three family friends were also preparing to leave for America, she knew this was her chance. This was it—the time had come!

So she packed her few belongings and spent as much time as she could with her baby daughter and her family. Her sister promised to bring Mañia in a year, but it was not to be. Karolina was never to see her first-born child again. Nor was she ever to see her mother, father, sister or younger brother again.

***

Mary Marcal Franek, Karolina's mother, was torn by her emotions. She wanted the best for her daughter Karolina—a good life with many opportunities to be happy. She also would have loved to live near her. She wanted to see Karolina marry and have a family. Mary looked forward to playing with all of her future grandchildren. Tears of sadness filled her life from this time on, because even though she had her little granddaughter, Mañia, to love and care for, she would never again experience her own daughter's laughter, smiles, tears, and joys.

Karolina's parents felt many fears about Karolina's plan to cross the Atlantic. And even though they wanted Karolina to be free to see the world and live her life, how could they deny the fear and sadness they felt in losing their daughter? There were so many unanswered questions. Where would Karolina live? Would she be safe—a beautiful twenty-year-old girl off on an adventure too big to imagine?

How, they wondered, did Karolina become such a spirited and determined young woman? That spirit *they* had always felt and had somehow repressed was now being released in Karolina's excitement and determination. Did they recognize themselves in her? Did they know that the vibrant spirit Karolina had acquired from them would live on in many generations to come?

Karolina waited until 1913. After paying a "head tax" of 20 koron in Bremen, Germany, on April 18, she boarded a great ship, *Kaiser Wilhelm der Grosse*, which was built for the Bremerhaven-to-New York run. Karolina was one of 1,970 passengers on this magnificent ship.[5]

The Kaiser Wilhelm der Grosse was the first four-funnel ship and the largest and fastest merchant ship in the world at this time. It moved so fast that the pounding Atlantic waves wore off the paint, which usually indicated a "record-breaking run." It was 655 feet long and 66 feet wide, weighed 14,349 tons, had twin propellers and "triple-expansion reciprocating steam engines." The three-story-tall pistons and cranks moved the great ship at twenty-three knots and crossed the Atlantic Ocean in less than six days.[7]

The *Kaiser Wilhelm der Grosse* was one of the most fashionable ships on the Atlantic. However, it was also known as "Rolling Billy" because it was top-heavy carrying New York's favorite cargo, full barrels of beer. With the advent of World War I one year after Karolina's trip, this great ship's final voyage was March 18, 1914. It was scuttled to avoid capture on August 26, 1914.[8]

So . . . if Karolina had left a year earlier, she might have been on the *Titanic*. And if she had left a year later, World War I could have prevented her from leaving Europe. It is by God's providence that she left when she did and that we are able to appreciate her spirit living in us in America today!

𝒦aiser 𝒲ilhelm der 𝒢rosse[6]
Courtesy GreatShips.net

Arriving in New York City with Julius Nemeth and several other family friends, Karolina stepped foot on Ellis Island on May 16, 1913. Soon she was on her way to Chicago to join her beloved Frank and the rest of her family and friends who had come before.

Eight months later, on January 19, 1914, with Karolina pregnant with twins, her friend, Ann Lichner, convinced her and Frank to marry. Two and one-half weeks later, on February 5, 1914, Karolina gave birth to twin girls, Veronica and Frances. At the christening of the twins, their godmother Ann accidentally switched the babies, and each was christened with the other's name! And once they were christened, the names stuck!

Soon, Karolina's sister in Czechoslovakia was making her plans to come to America and bring Mañia, Karolina's first-born daughter. Tragically, however, her sister slipped on ice and fell while pregnant. She died in Karvina.

On January 26, 1915, Karolina gave birth to their fourth daughter, Elizabeth. Karolina had several miscarriages in the year and a half that followed.

Then on July 17, 1916, their fifth daughter, Agnes, was born to this happy, growing family.

The 1916 family photo was taken on Agnes' christening day in St. John's Catholic Church in Chicago, Illinois. Although raised Catholic, later in life Karolina and most of her children converted to Protestant Christianity.

In the photo, baby Agnes is being held by her Aunt Agnes who is sitting next to her husband, Rudolph, Karolina's brother. Karolina is holding Elizabeth, and the fraternal twins are seated on the floor—Veronica in front of her father, Frank, and Frances to the right, in front of her uncle Rudolph. Don't they look grand and aristocratic? They were intelligent, hard working, and talented risk-takers in a country full of promise!

1916 Agnes' Christening Day

Part Two: Life in West Virginia

3

New Mine - New Life

Children are a reward from Him.
Psalm 127:3b

The move to West Virginia, in the mid-Appalachian region of eastern North America, offered a new opportunity to Frank and Karolina Grabiec. A boom in coal mining was brought about as World War I ended and reconstruction efforts began. In 1917, coal was discovered in the town of Galloway, and the Simpson Creek Collieries Company began operating the largest coal mine in northern West Virginia, putting out 2,700 tons a day! In 1918, Frank and Karolina decided to take advantage of this opportunity. They could live in the mining company housing and raise their children in the beautiful green countryside of the Appalachian Mountains.

The train took them as far as Flemington, and then the family boarded the small gasoline-powered, trolley-like train called the Jitney, which ran on the existing coal car tracks. As a wide-eyed young girl, Frances remembered riding lying down in the open-air Jitney late at night and looking up at the countless stars. As a child, she thought she had been riding in a covered wagon through the wilderness on their way to Galloway.

After settling into one of the mining company houses, the Grabiecs soon learned it would be a hard life. For miners and their families, hard work was expected and accepted as a way of life. Frank worked long hours in the mine, and Karolina worked long hours caring for the home and children and taking in laundry to make ends meet.

Hilltop View of Galloway, West Virginia

Frank started working at the Simpson Creek Collieries Company in August 1918. He earned approximately sixty-five cents a ton and was paid in scrip, which could only be used in the company store. If the family tried to shop anywhere else, the scrip was worthless. The miners had to trust the company regarding the amount of pay they earned each day. Then they were charged whatever the company store wanted for goods and services. They were at the mercy of the mining company. They had no recourse but to go along with whatever the company said was fair.

Since the company took out money for housing, tools, supplies, food, and fees, Frank was bringing home what amounted to pennies a day. Like most miners, the family had no insurance. They lived daily with the possibility that

Frank could be injured or killed from fires, explosions, methane gas, smoke, or cave-ins. He also was at risk for black lung from breathing coal dust, and other illnesses from the cold and dampness in the mines. In time, the union would help develop more fair and safe working conditions, but for now, the union dues were just an added expense for the Grabiec family.

There were no schools and no paved roads in the little mining town of Galloway in 1918. Most people did not have cars and few had a horse and buggy. When the Grabiec family had time to go somewhere, they usually walked along the paths or dirt roads. In an emergency they relied on getting a ride with a friend or neighbor who happened to have a car. The small train, "Ol' Jitney," as it was affectionately called, was the usual mode of transportation for longer distances. When the paved road was finally put in, it was made of concrete. For the road dedication, the little town held a big celebration and a parade with souvenir pencils thrown out for the children. The school, however, would not be built for four more years.

More babies brought joy and blessings to the Grabiec household. An old Polish tradition held that a man should marry a strong woman and have many children. Here in Galloway, four more blessed children were born to this growing family. Even though Karolina had been told how to abort her babies, she refused. She had a reverence for life and knew God was in control and would provide. Each child brought new joy and love into the home yet never healed the longing in Karolina's heart for her first child, Mañia, still in Czechoslovakia.

Karolina and her family shared a simple life. As the family grew, each person became more independent and yet less self-centered by sharing and helping one another. Even though the work was hard, Karolina enjoyed her children and every blessing God provided. Work in itself was a blessing—the joy of accomplishment and self sacrifice—the joy of giving more than receiving.

My mother Helen was the sixth child to be born to Frank and Karolina. She was born on December 17, 1919, and was the first of their children to be born in West Virginia. Her birth was not recorded by the doctor because, at this time, birth certificates needed to be taken by the family to be recorded by the county. (Later in life, my father had to write a letter to Barbour County to get the court to provide a certificate documenting my mother's birth.)

On the day Helen was born, Karolina handed her to Frances, who was

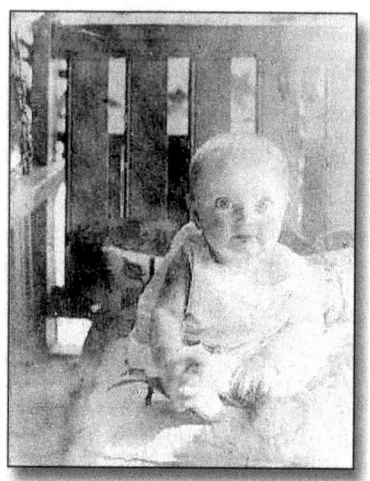

Baby Helen

five at the time, and said, "Here, Frances. She is yours to take care of." Frances and Helen became very close and remained close all their lives. (Even as an adult, Helen said she still felt like Frances was her mentor.)

When her first boy was born on June 2, 1921, Karolina said to the midwife, "Did I have a boy? Name him 'Frank'!" Thus she named her first-born son after his father.

Karolina gave birth to her second son fourteen months later on August 24, 1922. He was named Joseph David, after Karolina's father, Joseph, and her dedicated and caring company doctor, Dr. S. David Hays.

On one occasion the family posed for a photo in front of their company house. This is the only photo ever found of Frank Sr. with his family. In this

1923 Grabiec Family
Frank Sr., Elizabeth, Agnes, Frances, Helen, Veronica,
Frank Jr., Karolina, Joseph

1923 photo, Karolina is holding baby Joseph, about ten months old, and she is pregnant with Annie.

Frank Jr. remembers that one day the family had to appear in court for some reason. He was too young to remember what it was for. He does remember he had to wear a dress, which was customary for little boys at that time. When he protested, his sisters told him they would all be fed after their court appearance, which encouraged him to comply. As it turned out they were not fed, but their court appearance was over.

When Annie was born on March 21, 1924, Elizabeth (now called Betty) was so excited that she fell down the steps of the big two-story boarding house they rented at the time. This added to the excitement of the day! Annie was the ninth and last child to be born to Karolina and Frank Sr.

All the brothers and sisters shared a close bond with their mother and with each other. They needed each other, and throughout their lives they shared the good times and the bad—they were always there for each other.

4

Seasons of Love

Let it be the hidden person of the heart, with the imperishable quality of a gentle and quiet spirit, which is precious in the sight of God.
1 Peter 3:4 (NAS)

Karolina's gentle and quiet spirit was overshadowed at times by the problems and chaos of life. But she knew where her strength came from and persevered in doing what was right in spite of her difficulties.

Fondness and fear were two other conflicting emotions for the Grabiec children. My mother had a close bond with her father. Their birthdays were two days apart—his December 15 and hers December 17. When she was a child, he bought clothes with matching shoes or hats for her when he could. And she loved his music. To her it was magical to hear him play the violin, clarinet and flute. He wanted his children to learn to appreciate good music, so every day they were to quietly listen as he played classical pieces. I am sure this is where my mother's passion for music was born.

Agnes also loved her father yet feared him. Every Saturday she watched him play the violin on the front porch as he looked up at the night sky. She loved to hear him play, but because she feared him, she sat inside the house behind the window, peeking through the curtain as she listened.

She was afraid of him because he had been violently angry at her in the past. One day when she tried to open a jar of grease, she spilled it. "Did you open the lard and spill it all over?" he yelled. She was so scared she ran out the door and hid under the porch. She remembered sitting there and her mother calling her, but she would not come out.

Another time, when she had trouble reading in school, he punished her by not giving her a cookie even though everyone else had gotten one. This incident left her feeling broken-hearted and affected her for the rest of her life. Sadness filled her face as she talked with me about her father. She never forgot that feeling of fear and cried telling about these memories.

However, Agnes fondly remembers her mother, Karolina. "She was the sweetest person I ever knew," Agnes recounts. "When I was lonely, she knew of it before I did. I enjoyed life because she was so good. You couldn't find a better person. She had a heart of gold. My best memory is the way she taught me and made me listen." As she thought about her mother in Heaven, she looked up and called out to her, saying: "I want you to know who the most precious mother is. You are the most important person in my life!" Then to me she added, "Some day I will be with my mother. I see her—I do. I see the things that she has done. I'm proud of her . . . I'll always be proud."

The Garden

Fun and food were usually found daily by the Grabiec children living in Galloway. Besides having chickens and a cow for milk, they all loved their garden, even though the younger ones were too little to work it. The garden area was on a hill between the stilts under the shed of the "lower house," as they called the company house. As the seasons changed, the children's activities in the garden area changed. In the summer they planted the garden, and in the winter they would slide over the snow-covered hill on flattened boxes.

Karolina told her children they could do whatever they wanted to after school when their daily chores were finished. Agnes remembers how they ran to their garden where they had planted seeds of beans and vegetables like tomatoes, carrots, and onions. "We had everything we needed and more," she muses. They carefully watered each day and tended the little plants as they popped up. They loved their garden so much they would often stay out late at night. "Once we stayed out until two o'clock in the morning in the moonlight," she remembers. It was springtime, and under a full moon they were planting potatoes–the "peelings with three eyes," as my cousin Carole Jane explained it.

When food was scarce, the friendly neighbors of Galloway pitched in. Agnes remembers the "pound party" they gave the Grabiec family one night. Each person brought a "pound" of food. They brought potatoes and lots of canned goods. So much was piled on the table that it fell on the floor. Agnes remembers thinking, "What wonderful neighbors we have–to do something like that for our mother. And what a wonderful country we live in."

One of Agnes' fondest memories is of Karolina making fresh potato pancakes. She knew that whenever they had potato pancakes, they were full for the night! Agnes can still see her mother "gratin' potatoes on an old-fashioned grater." One day when Agnes was too young to be in school, she saw Karolina cut her finger on the grater. Agnes wrapped up Karolina's finger for her and proudly finished grating the potatoes. She says she will never forget that moment no matter how young she was or how old she gets!

Karolina's children remember what a good cook she was. She could make a delicious, filling meal with very little. She made homemade noodles and dumplings and lots of good soups with vegetables and chicken or whatever she had.

In the beautiful green hills of West Virginia the family always could find something good to eat. My mother and her brothers and sisters remembered picking blackberries–filling up their buckets so they would have enough to eat as well as to make jams and jellies. Blackberry jam became one of my mother's favorites. Two sweet neighbor ladies, Mrs. Benda and Mrs. Katula, owned apple orchards nearby and told the children they could pick up as many apples as they wanted that had fallen on the ground. With these Karolina made wonderful apple *kolaczki* (we pronounce it "ko wä' che") (rolls filled with jams and other fillings), jams, and apple dumplings. She canned as many apples as she could for winter.

Not only was she a good cook but Karolina also made clothes for the children. She made comfortable play clothes and made their school dresses out of flour-sack cloth with beautiful prints, Agnes remembers. The children always felt they had nice clothes to wear to school. When shoes were bought, they were saved for school. There was no need for lots of clothes—just a few warm ones for winter and cool ones for the summer. They were happy, sharing what they had, and Karolina was good at mending and patching to keep the clothes looking good.

Young Frances

Karolina's calm nature helped the family feel secure. With eight children, Karolina just had to trust God to protect them all, and she did the best she could within her circumstances. She never lost her temper, Joseph remembers. As a little boy, when he did something wrong she never yelled. She put him on her lap and said in a soft voice, "Joseph, you know you shouldn't behave like that." He felt so bad it would make him want to behave better. Karolina did not say much, but when she did, she spoke in a soft voice. She had a strong, quiet spirit.

Young Betty

When Helen teased Agnes by putting her cold feet on her one night, Agnes screamed. Karolina said, "OK, Helen, that's enough." That's all she had to say to make Helen stop. Karolina disciplined with few words, so when she did speak, her children respected her wishes.

Years later when someone complained about a child's behavior, I remember Grandmother Karolina saying, "Ah! Kids is kids!" in her broken English. Cousin Audrey remembers when her mother, Veronica (now called Verna), was angry with her, Karolina said, "You can't put a cow's head on a calf!" She knew it took time and patience to teach children.

Grandma Karolina showed us how "calm is strength, and anger is weakness."[9] With God's help she demonstrated a quiet strength within herself and thus was strong for others.

5

Days of Danger and Delight

Do not be afraid, for I am with you.
Genesis 26:24b

Living in Galloway the Grabiec children experienced danger and pain as well as many happy days of fun and adventure. **Gashed to the bone** by broken glass–Agnes remembers it well. Since Karolina had to take in laundry to supplement the family income, all the children learned how to help. It was Agnes' job to tote heavy buckets of water from the nearby pump. Walking barefoot as she liked to do, she often cut her feet. One day she was at the pump with her sister Frances and cut her foot severely, this time on broken glass sticking out of the mud. Frank Jr. later found the broken Coke bottle which had been partially exposed by the rain.

When Frances saw Agnes' bleeding foot, gashed to the bone, she screamed so loudly that Karolina sent Betty up to see what had happened. Betty quickly helped Agnes get home, and Karolina, seeing the bone exposed, shouted, "Get the white bed sheet off the line!" She tore it into strips and bound Agnes' foot together using about half of the white sheet, Agnes remembers.

Dr. Hays was called but could not come because he was already on a call. He said he would come out the next day to see what he could do. As she saw his horse and buggy approaching the next day, Agnes said, "Ma! Soak my foot, so the stuck bandages won't pull it open again!" So they soaked and carefully unwrapped her torn foot and covered it with a clean sheet to keep the flies off. When Dr. Hays got there and saw the seriousness of the injury, he apologized for not coming the day before. He had been waiting to deliver a baby and could not leave.

To distract little Agnes from the pain of stitching the gaping wound, Dr. Hays gave her two quarters to hold in her little hands. He said, "I have no pain medicine, so when I have to put the needle into your flesh to stitch it, just bite on these coins." The coins were so precious to her that instead of biting them she squeezed them in her hands as tightly as she could for each stitch. Dr. Hays had to put in eight stitches that way.

"I have never seen such a brave little girl," Dr. Hays said to Agnes and her mother. As he was finishing up, Agnes remembers he called over his shoulder, "Mrs. Grabiec, do you need any eggs? I have a carton of eggs I want to give you." She laughed, saying, "Instead of me paying you, you want to give me a carton of eggs?" Agnes said it was the biggest box of eggs she had ever seen. "We ate eggs for a long time," she remembers.

For several weeks Agnes had to be pulled around in a doll's wooden wagon. She laughs when she remembers the town rumor that "one of the Grabiec girls cut her leg off!" But her mother was not amused. "Agnes, you can't keep cutting your feet. I need you to help with the chores!" Karolina admonished.

A fragmented fingertip was just one of Frank Jr.'s childhood injuries. The gears of the old wringer washing machine had looked fascinating to him as a little boy. "I just wanted to touch them," he said as he pointed inquisitively with his index finger, as he must have done that day. "As I stuck my finger into the gears, the tip of it was mashed up," Frank Jr. recalls, "and Dr. Hays was called again." (My sister, Nancy, remembers our mother was always worried when children were near our old wringer washing machine. This must have been the reason.)

"Dr. Hays always patched up the Grabiecs," Frank Jr. said. He became a very special person to the Grabiec family. We all had such respect for him; he was like a godfather."

Electrical wires which hung overhead for powering the movement of the coal cars also enticed the children. As a little girl Agnes remembers thinking, "I wonder what would happen if I grabbed those wires." Standing with both feet on the track, she grabbed the wires with both hands. She got a shock and luckily was able to let go. She found out that day what would happen and never forgot it!

On another day, Agnes' little brother Joe picked up a long stick and announced, "I'm a trolley!" as he stood on the track and touched the wire with the stick. Zap! The shock knocked him flat. He woke up wondering, "What happened?"

Joe also remembers hitching a ride on a slow-moving coal train when he was too young to be in school. "The train kept going and going," he said, "and the engineer yelled, 'You better get off. You're a long way from home and you have to walk back.'" So he jumped off and remembers it was a long walk home along the tracks. "The scariest part was walking over the open spaces between the ties on the bridge." Joe still remembers the feeling of fear he had then as a little boy over seventy-five years ago.

A midnight miracle is not easily forgotten. Frank Jr. remembers that in 1925 when he was four, his baby sister, one-year-old Annie, had pneumonia.

Galloway Road

The children gathered around her with their mother and watched her all night by candlelight. They watched Karolina hold and rub the tiny, skinny, naked baby. They were sure Annie was going to die. But she didn't! How she survived, they didn't know. Years later as they grew in their faith in God, they understood that they had witnessed a miracle!

The woodland wilds in West Virginia brought delight to the Grabiec children. Even though they were warned about the bobcats and black bear, their spirit of adventure lived on in their never-ending love of the upland forests. When the youngest were too little to work or go to school, they loved playing in the lush nearby woods, climbing over fallen trees and inspecting mushrooms. Later their mother would teach them how to identify the good mushrooms to eat, but for now they were just having fun.

Helen loved to talk about playing in the woods as a child with Frances. Frances described how she would tie one end of a rope around baby Helen's waist and the other end to a tree so Helen would not get lost. Then Frances was free to run and play nearby.

As they got older they enjoyed making up games, improvising toys, and imagining things. Near the ponds they would capture frogs and green salamanders and chase wild geese. Yet, as a little girl, my mother became afraid of geese because a large one chased *her* and pulled at her dress one spring morning, Agnes remembers, laughing.

On another day while Helen ran through the woods her little foot almost stepped on a snake! It could easily have been a garter snake or a water snake, but she had been warned of the deadly timber rattlesnakes and copperheads. She screamed and kept running. She screamed so loudly they could hear her all the way home. Karolina wondered what the screaming was all about this time and sent Agnes to check on her. "All that screaming was kind of hard to take, but we rescued her," Agnes remembers. Helen was terrified of snakes for the rest of her life.

The birds were special to Helen. They must have exhibited the freedom of spirit she felt. She remembered the red-breasted robins and the red cardinals that her mother, Karolina, loved. As an adult, Mom always had bird feeders in her front and back yards which brought back pleasant memories.

Smoke and slag from the coal mines of Galloway made an attraction a coal-miner's young son could not resist. As Frank Jr. walked across the smoldering slag piles, he was fascinated by the cable cars overhead. They were filled with slag and moved along a cable supported by wooden trestles between two hills. He watched as the buckets tipped and poured out waste rock onto the growing mountain of slag. Blue smoke filled the air from the fires below. He remembers the constant smell of stinking smoke in the air and the grass occasionally catching fire with the heat. He now realizes how dangerous it was to be playing there. He knows just one slip and he could have fallen into a crevasse of hot smoldering slag.

Tin cups and toys kept the children busy in their free time. One day some of the kids were feeling especially ornery, Agnes remembers, giggling. It was payday for the miners, and several of the older kids thought it would be fun to have little Annie and Helen hold tin cups, wait near where the miners were cashing their checks, and ask for their change. I wonder what Karolina's reaction was when they brought the coins home that day!

The Grabiecs remembered many of the wonderful times they shared playing together. One of their favorite memories is when they used sardine cans to make miniature cable cars. They filled them with dirt, slowly raised them up with string, and moved them across string "cables." Then they tipped them over and dumped them out, just like the cable cars they had watched overhead. They improvised many toys in this way, creating and re-creating interesting and unique playthings. All their lives the Grabiecs would be creative—often making something from what seemed like nothing. The spirit of invention and improvisation they developed lives on in Karolina's descendants today.

Hooky, haunts, and jaunts made for exciting childhood adventures. Frank Jr. remembers the day he played hooky from school. He can still remember standing on top of the hill, looking down at the schoolhouse, thinking, "That's where *I'm* supposed to be!" But his determined spirit of adventure enticed him to go tramping through the woods, looking at puddles of water, bugs, and other interesting things in nature. One day he even got the courage to explore a few hundred feet into a coal mine where he had been told never to go. As he went deeper into the mine, he got scared and ran out!

He must have shared the experience with his sisters because one day Agnes' curiosity made her want to see inside a coal mine also. So her father took her and another sister for their first peek into a coal mine. She remembers it was a terribly dark and scary place!

Nearby Simpson Creek, on the other side of the railroad tracks, was another fascinating place for the Grabiec children to play. They had to watch out for quicksand and snakes, and the water was yellow with sulfur from the mines. The sulfur's rotten egg smell filled the air, but they didn't mind, Frank Jr. remembers. He recalls an old song about that creek with the yellow water– "Simpson Creek Will Never Run Clear Again."

With the wet velvety moss and algae growing on the rocks, walking beside the creek was dangerous. One day while walking home from school the kids decided to cool off in the inviting water. In his excitement and rush to get into the water with his big sisters, Frank Jr. ran so fast he slipped on the mossy rocks and fell in. Agnes yelled for Betty to grab him! Just in time Betty grabbed him by the collar and saved him from being swept away.

Another adventure the Grabiecs loved was going to town on the "short hops" train. "Old Jitney" went to Fairmont, Clarksburg, and other neighboring towns in the morning and back to Galloway in the evening. The Grabiecs loved the excitement of traveling to town, staying all day if they wanted to, and meeting the friendly people of West Virginia.

Miners' rallies brought even more excitement to Galloway. When the union was organizing the miners, Frank Jr. remembers as a little boy "being drug off to union meetings for hours and hours." It was important to the miners that their kids understood what was going on and learned how to fight for better working conditions. Frank Jr. remembers the meetings often turned militant. Eventually the unions were approved by President Franklin D. Roosevelt, however, and became more accepted in the community.

At one union rally, my mother remembered her dad placed her up on a box when she was about five or six and had her sing a coal-miners' union song– a song which she never forgot. Even in her eighties she remembered and could sing every word.

Frank Jr. also remembers hearing the "boom" around town of dynamite exploding. "Was that from the mines?" I asked him. "No, it was usually dynamite stolen from the mines by people wanting to use it for celebrations or other purposes," he said. While visiting with the locals in Galloway, I learned what one of the "other purposes" was. Many years ago an unfaithful wife had used dynamite to murder her sleeping husband so she could be free. Such tragedies are still talked about in the little town of Galloway today.

Frank Jr. remembers sitting in the cozy living room of their home when he was a boy. He breathed in the wonderful smell of his mother's baking. She was making her delicious Polish *kolaczki*, which were small rolls filled with fruits, cheese, or nuts and baked to a golden brown. They were topped with *posipka*, a mouth-watering, crumbly butter-sugar-flour topping. He remembers just sitting there, waiting for his warm biscuit and watching the beautiful snow falling outside.

FLASH!

All of a sudden a bright light filled the window, illuminating millions of falling white snowflakes! How beautiful the scene was!

But what was it?

In disparate contrast to the beauty of the brightly-lit falling snowflakes, the beam was a union searchlight piercing the peaceful scene, looking for strike-breaker "scabs." How quickly the dreamy beauty of the scene was perverted by the passions of men.

The mining accident of 1925 brought another series of changes in the lives of the Grabiecs. My grandfather, Frank Sr., was the victim of another severe head injury–this time in the mine. The scream of the whistle sounded the emergency, and Frank Sr. was one of those removed from the mine. Agnes remembers when the mining authorities brought him home to Karolina. Karolina wrapped his head with pillow feathers to seal the wound. She did the best she could since there was no hospital and no emergency facilities.

After this second head injury Frank Sr. could no longer work. Karolina hired someone to come each day to care for him since she had to take on even more work as well as take care of the children.

Frank Sr.'s violent headaches and pain increased. Instead of being the gentle man the children once knew, he had more violent fits of anger and jealousy. He flew into a rage if a man even looked at Karolina. During these rages, Karolina told Verna and Frances to take the younger children to the woods to hide out in safety. At times like this, Karolina held baby Annie tightly and quietly prayed.

These and many other exciting and often dangerous adventures created unforgettable memories of West Virginia for Karolina's children. It was easy for them to play and be free-spirited, even as their mother taught them the values of hard work, persistence, and family unity. They shared many good times as well as difficulties and hardships, but they were never alone. "God is above us," Karolina reminded her children often.

6

The Real Survivors

Sorrowful, yet always rejoicing; poor, yet making many rich; having nothing, and yet possessing everything.
2 Corinthians 6:10

The real survivors were those who could endure the difficult and trying times in Galloway. Over time, as they matured, the Grabiecs became more aware of the significance of these events which were vividly etched in their memories.

School days in Galloway began in 1923 when, after four years of waiting, a school was finally built. When it was completed, the four older children all started the first grade together–the twins, Verna and Frances at age nine, Betty,

Galloway School

age eight, and Agnes, age seven. Later as they each turned six, Helen, Frank, and Joseph also started school in Galloway.

Excited to finally be able to go to school, the children walked across the tracks and up the road to the schoolhouse. Frances described how they would often run underneath the slow-moving train cars loaded with coal so they could get to school on time.

Frank Jr.'s first experience in first grade, however, was a miserable one for him. He walked in, was handed a piece of chalk, and was told to write his name on the board. He remembers just staring at the chalk, staring at the board, and thinking, "I don't know what to do!" Having grown up in a Polish-speaking family, he did not speak English. This was a totally new experience for him. He had never been in a classroom before. He had no idea of what was expected. Poor little guy! What a lost feeling that must have been!

Another embarrassing moment was when Verna tried to make friends. She had said, "W'a's you name?" and was made fun of by the English-speaking children. Embarrassed and upset, she told her father of the incident. He told her sternly, "Learn English!"

At that time there was no special program for non-English-speaking children. But they learned fast in what would be described today as a type of "immersion" program. They had to just get in there and learn English by listening and using new words every day.

A happy memory for the Grabiec children was the beautiful Christmas pageant the school put on one winter. The teachers arranged a gift exchange and a wonderful musical program with costumes. The program was so large it had to be performed in a rented facility in town. Karolina made the girls beautiful white dresses with angels' wings. Little Agnes was extremely excited and impressed. Some of the songs they sang were "Silent Night," "Oh, Little Town of Bethlehem," and "Oh, Come All Ye Faithful." She remembers one song had the words, "See the little snowflakes falling from the sky." The bright lights, beautiful angel costumes, and Christmas music remain in her memory today as if it all happened only yesterday!

During the gift exchange, however, Frances did not receive a present.

The child who drew her name had not brought one, so her teacher gave her a little toy peanut that opened up with a tiny baby doll inside. She loved that toy so much she took it home and hid it in the rafters of the house so no one would take it or lose it. When she went to find it years later, it was gone because the old houses had been removed.

One of Frank's good memories of school was when it was his turn to ring the school bell. He had to go into the small, dark closet that housed the rope and pull as hard as he could. He loved ringing the school bell.

Frank Jr. also never forgot the fun and adventures he had trekking to and from school every day. He had many opportunities to play, laugh, and talk . . . and get into mischief!

One incident involved Frank Jr. trying to hitch a ride to school on a truck. The driver was going in the direction of the school, so Frank grabbed on to the truck tailgate, his feet running faster and faster as the truck sped up. Eventually the stinging from the friction of the street caused him to finally let go. He tumbled down onto the cement road and got "really beat up," he recalls. This incident happened just before the family's move from Galloway. Frank Jr. remembers being on the train afterwards and looking at all those scratches still on his hands and arms.

One cold winter day as young Frank Jr. left for the long walk home from school, he *really* had to go the bathroom but wanted to wait until he got home. The wait was just too long for a little boy, and he had an "accident." It was such a cold day that his pants were frozen solid on his legs by the time he got home.

A frightful time for all the children while in school was hearing the mine whistle blasting the announcement of an emergency. It usually signaled a disaster of some kind. Frank Jr. remembers they were to just wait at school for the news and were usually not told much. When they were dismissed for the day everyone went home to find out what had happened. The children and the entire town knew the feeling of panic as it could be one of their fathers, brothers, sons, neighbors, or other loved ones endangered this time.

One fateful day, perhaps due to stress, worry, and jealousy, Frank Grabiec Sr. had an emotional breakdown. He got a gun and started shooting at the house and the neighborhood, Frank Jr. recalls. Everyone was afraid—especially Karolina. All the kids quickly escaped to the neighbor's house, but Annie, the youngest, was asleep in her crib. Karolina was terrified of what he might do. But instead of doing what she feared, he went in, warmed baby Annie's bottle, and fed her.

Early the next morning Frank Sr. was arrested. When the authorities came to get him, he was in his long johns. Frank Jr. remembers the vision of his father, about 5'3" tall and 130 pounds. My mother was sad to see her handsome father taken away. "Let's go, Frank," they said. They took him away in an unmarked, gray-green Chevrolet sedan. From that day on, Karolina alone had the burden of raising her eight children. They remained fatherless for the rest of their lives.

Dr. Hays felt sorry for Karolina and her children and testified that Frank Sr. was mentally ill—saying he was worse than he actually was. The authorities then sent him to Weston, West Virginia, to the mental hospital. For many years most of his family members did not see him. When my mother visited him in the hospital, she remembered he had a little patch of garden and he was getting better. At one point, Karolina paid $75 for an attorney to try to get him released, but he remained in the hospital for many years.

With Frank Sr. now gone, the Grabiecs had lost the "privilege" of living in the company housing. Karolina decided to move her family to what was known as the "big white house on the hill." She rented out any extra rooms to miners and provided their meals. Frank Jr. remembers being sad to leave the house where he was born.

"The big white house on the hill" had been built years earlier by Joseph Piaza who was nicknamed "Groundhog" because he had started underground, building his two-story house overlooking Galloway. The older girls were excited about having more space in this big house, but Frank Jr. remembers the miners constantly bossing him and his brother and sisters around. "They ruled us like we were *their* kids," he remembers. He also remembers being amazed at how the miners, covered in soot and coal dust, could "bathe" in just tubs of cold water on the front porch before they could come in the house.

Agnes told the story of how the miners passed by their house every day going to get water from the pump near the front porch. One evening she and Betty, in a fit of good humor, thought they could scare the miners. They held up a white sheet in the window hoping the miners would think a ghost haunted the house (Agnes giggles as she remembers this childish antic). For a few weeks after that, the girls thought that the miners *did* avoid walking past their house!

Working diligently, the family tried to make enough money to stay and manage the two-story boarding house in Galloway. Karolina took in more laundry, and the three older girls cleaned more neighboring houses. Karolina washed clothes using a washboard, a round tub, and brown Felsnaphtha soap. That soap made the clothes smell so fresh, Agnes remembers. Agnes toted the buckets of water, and Frances had the hated job of washing the black, dirty socks. But Karolina had taught her children how to work hard. She taught them to bring home every penny. The money would add up and be enough to buy a bottle of milk or a loaf of bread.

Many Polish families as well as families of other nationalities lived, worked, and helped each other survive in Galloway. One of the neighbors they loved was Mrs. Katula. Agnes remembers that Mrs. Katula had a large oven where she made lots of good bread which she shared with the Grabiecs. Mrs. Katula and her daughter Anna were good friends to Karolina and her family.

A Westside shanty in the valley near Simpson Creek was the Grabiec family's third and final home in Galloway. The area was also known as "Little Italy." The shanty was a roughly made wood building with spaces between the boards. "It was a 25' by 30' shanty at most," Frank Jr. recalls. It had two or three small rooms with no electricity. They remember having no electric lights, heating, or warm water. They tried to keep warm with a coal-burning stove and their mother's homemade *pierzynas*. Karolina covered many of the spaces between the slats with cardboard to stop the cold air from blowing through.

There was no indoor plumbing, so they used outhouses and hauled water for bathing and cooking. They had two water pumps outside—one near the house for drinking and cooking and one farther away for cleaning and washing. Occasionally when it rained, Karolina and the children collected the rain water in tubs and buckets. It was such nice, soft water for bathing when there was enough to fill the large round tub. The children were bathed outside on the lawn in full view of all the neighbors, Frank Jr. remembers—the older children first and the little ones (usually the dirtiest ones!) last.

But the rain was not always kind. In the middle of the night on Saturday, August 1, 1927, after days of pouring rain, Simpson Creek flooded. The torrential rains washed away their precious garden. This was very disheartening for the family, but they were grateful to be safe. Other families lost their homes, yet they were thankful no one was killed in the devastating flood.

About fifty feet from the front of the shanty were the railroad tracks with coal cars moving back and forth during the day. As the trains rumbled by, the children picked up the coal that fell from the heavily-laden cars. At times they yelled for the train crew to throw some coal down for them. They used whatever they could collect to heat their home and cook their meals. They worked hard to be able to eat, keep warm, and keep up with the rent.

Across the road from the Westside Shanties was a cemetery. One day Frank Jr. saw the beautiful wild flowers and decided to crawl under the front gate and pick some. As he was crawling back under the gate, a girl saw him and yelled, "I'm gonna tell, and you're gonna get it! You shouldn't be stealing flowers!" Scared to death, Frank Jr. also felt very embarrassed. He wasn't stealing flowers—they were wild flowers. But he never forgot that horrible feeling from her insinuating that he was stealing.

Mañia, her firstborn, was always in Karolina's heart. When Karolina wrote to her mother, Mary, in Czechoslovakia to make plans for Mañia to come to America, Mary responded, "Karolina, you have enough work caring for eight children." Her mother was right. Mañia would be much better off staying with her grandparents in Czechoslovakia, Karolina conceded sadly. What a shock it would have been for Mañia to come to their little home in the coal-mining town of Galloway and be so poor! "I agree," she wrote to her mother. "Mañia is 100% better off there than my eight hungry children here in West Virginia." But Karolina never forgot Mañia.[10]

7

Tragedies and Trials

We were harassed at every turn—conflicts on the outside, fears within.
2 Corinthians 7:5b

Haunting Memories

Stories of more tragedies and trials in West Virginia emerged from conversations I had with Grabiec family members and their Galloway neighbors.

The ax murder in the late 1920s has not been forgotten in Galloway. Those few who were there are now in their eighties and nineties and still remember how it happened. The story was avoided in Grabiec family discussions for years but was never forgotten by the Grabiec children.

They remembered fifteen-year-old Katie and her father, Joe Piaza. After the Grabiecs had moved out of his house, Mr. Piaza rented an upper-level room to Joe Grobowski, a twenty-nine-year-old bachelor, and a lower-level room to Rudy Kusick, a bachelor from Poland. He then had sent for his fourteen-year-old daughter, Katie, to be the housekeeper for him. As time went on, Joe, the upstairs tenant, wanted to marry Katie, but she was attracted to Rudy.

The following year, as the mine work slacked off, Mr. Piaza went out of town to look for work. While her father was out of town, Katie and Rudy decided to go to the courthouse to get a marriage license. Joe, seeing them walking together, became extremely jealous and angry and resolved to kill her. He went to the general store and told the owner he wanted to buy two steaks to surprise Katie by cooking them for her dinner. He also said he wanted to buy the sharpest ax in the store. He bought them, went back to the house, and waited for her to come home.

In town, Katie and Rudy found the courthouse was closed and, disappointed, walked home. When they got home, Katie went into her kitchen, and Rudy went to his downstairs apartment. Furious at this point, Joe came out of the attic and, in a rage, attacked Katie with the ax. She fought to defend herself but did not have a chance. From downstairs Rudy heard the scuffling. By the time he got upstairs, Joe had decapitated her. "I killed Katie! She do nothing to me no more! I don't need ax no more," he confessed to Rudy in his broken English as he dropped the ax and ran into the woods.

The town was in shock. Young Frank Jr. and some of the other kids heard the news and Frank ran over to see what had happened. All alone, he remembers slowly climbing up the stairs of the house he had formerly lived in. And there was the body. He saw all the blood and her legs and torso. Today he is glad he did not look further to see her decapitated head.

Frank Jr. remembers watching the authorities and volunteers searching the woods for days until Joe was finally caught. He was put into that same unmarked, gray-green Chevrolet sedan. As the Chevrolet drove down the road, Frank Jr. remembers the way the murderer looked at him and the other kids watching from the street. He will never forget those staring eyes looking straight at him!

The authorities had difficulty finding Katie's father to tell him the bad news. They later located him in Bluefield, West Virginia, and at the news, he passed out.

Joe was taken to jail. While there, he took wires out of a broom and hung himself. It was said that the blood stains could never be entirely removed from that beautiful "big white house on the hill."

The Morgantown rescue of young Frances still stirs apprehension of "what could have been" in some Grabiec hearts today. When Frances was about ten, she was always ready for an adventure. One day an elderly man asked her to get permission from her mother to come help him take care of his wheelchair-bound wife. Karolina gave her permission and off she went. Later, when the couple moved to Morgantown 40 miles away, they took Frances with them. They were not abusive to her, but they did not tell Karolina where they lived and did not mail Frances' letters home to her mother.

After many days with no word from Frances, Karolina became worried. She knew the elderly couple had moved to Morgantown but did not know where and did not know why she had not heard from her daughter. A neighbor offered to drive Karolina to Morgantown to help her find Frances. So early one day at 5:00 a.m. Karolina gave the children a stern warning to stay home, be safe, and not to touch the matches. When she was sure they understood, she left.

Meanwhile, in Morgantown, Frances had been thinking of running away to try to find her way home. She thought that she could follow the train tracks all the way home. She did not realize, however, that there were train tracks branching out in several directions from Morgantown, and she probably would have become lost.

In Morgantown, Karolina and her neighbor searched all day. As she rode around in the car, Karolina prayed that Frances would climb a fencepost or a tree so she could find her. Toward evening, Frances *did* climb a cherry tree. She could hear a car coming and wanted to see it.

As she watched the car slowly coming up the dirt road, Frances saw her mother's head sticking out of the car window with her hair in that familiar bun.

She screamed, "Ma! Ma!" Karolina heard her screams, turned, and saw Frances up in the cherry tree! She quickly got out and yelled, "Get in the car!"

The elderly man and his wife begged Karolina to let her stay because they needed her. "You can't take her!" they pleaded.

"I *will* take her; she's my daughter!" Karolina asserted.

They promised they would allow her to write home and receive letters. But Karolina was firm. *"Never again!"* she said angrily.

When they got home to Galloway late that night, Karolina was relieved to see that all her children were safe and sound. She cried tears of joy and thankfulness! "Frances was so glad to be home, she didn't know how to act," Agnes remembers. "She was just so thankful to be home with her family again."

***

Bootlegging to survive was not uncommon in poor mining towns in America during Prohibition.

One day in the mid-1990s, Aunt Verna, Aunt Frances, Uncle Joe, and my mother all sat in Frances' living room reminiscing about their childhood days in West Virginia.

"Who hid the whiskey bottles under the house?" asked Verna.

A hand immediately went up. "I did!" smiled Frances. "It was me!"

***

Yes, Frances had been the smallest in size, and at her young age she was the best one to quickly dart under the house to hide the moonshine. To feed her eight children, Karolina learned how to barrel and ferment the oat mash, boil the brew in her oval pot with its copper lid sealed with bread dough, condense it through a copper coiled tube, and collect the liquor into gallon bottles. She used a hydrometer to test the strength of the brew, Frank Jr. recalls. At that point it was 180 proof whiskey. She browned sugar in a frying pan and added it to the whiskey for color. Then she thinned it with water to 80 proof. Of course, this was during the Prohibition years, and one day as my mother was singing, Karolina was afraid it would attract attention. She scolded, "Helen, stop that singing! You'll get us arrested!"

On another day young Frances caught Mr. Popovitch peeking through the spaces between the boards in the shanty. She was so startled and angry that she spit in his eye! This, and Karolina's rejection of his amorous advances, angered him. So he reported Karolina's bootlegging to the local authorities and led them to her house. They found the whiskey, smashed up the bottles, and left.

On another raid, as an officer arrived at the house, Frank Jr. remembers the younger children sobbing in fear, "They're gonna take us to the poorhouse!" The officers searched the property and found the fermenting barrel of mash under a hatch in the floorboards, covered with a rug and stove in the center of the house. The officers carried the barrel out of the house, and watching from the woods, Frank Jr. saw them dump the beautiful bright yellow mash out onto the ground. In contrast, he remembers the awful fermenting smell. When the officers threatened to arrest Karolina for bootlegging, she said, "OK, I'll go with you. But you'll have to feed and take care of my eight children. They depend on me alone!" Realizing this, they did not arrest her. One officer put a pint in his back pocket and gave her a suggestion. "Just call it 'home brew,'" he advised.

Stories of the city captivated the minds of the young Grabiecs and their mother. Karolina's friend Ann Lichner told her to come back to Chicago where Ann's son, Al, could help her find a job with the railroad, and she would not have to work so hard. For the children it was exciting when Al came to visit and told them about life in Chicago. While visiting the Grabiecs in Galloway, Al was challenged by a large log in the yard and was determined to stay until he could split it up as firewood for them. It took longer than he had anticipated, and the kids were thrilled that he had to stay longer and share more stories of life in the big city.

Finding a way out of poverty took determination and faith. Mr. Popovitch, the man who led the authorities to bust Karolina's bootlegging, probably hoped she was now desperate, and again he pressured her to marry him. He advised her to put her four youngest children in an orphanage while the four oldest girls continue to work. Furious at the suggestion of giving up four of her children, Karolina asked him, "Which of my fingers should I cut off? And if I did give up four of my children, why would I need *you?*" Karolina retorted.

My mother was one of the four youngest children, and at her young age she thought that going to an orphanage meant some kind of an adventure. She remembered feeling disappointed when they did not get to go. She had no concept of what going to an orphanage really meant at that time. Later in life she realized why her mother had refused Mr. Popovitch's proposal and was thankful.

As her older girls became young women and the work became more difficult for Karolina, she realized she needed to move her family out of Galloway. In 1928, Karolina's brother Rudy sent for the older girls to come live with him and his family in Chicago. He told Karolina the girls could earn $1.00 a day, $7 a week, working as maids for the wealthy families of Chicago. After finishing six years of schooling in Galloway, fourteen-year-old Frances was the first to take the long trip on the train to Chicago. Verna and Betty soon followed.

Karolina later described the day she "escaped" from her ardent pursuer and finally moved the rest of her family out of Galloway.

"Leave me alone!" Karolina told him, as he pressured her.

He didn't, of course, so she thought she would discourage him by suggesting he shave off his beard—but he did! Surprised by his determination, she now knew he would come back for her. She decided this would be a great time to leave town! The three older girls had already left for Chicago, and even though she had little money, she got her children onto the train to leave West Virginia for good.

Mr. Popovitch heard Karolina was leaving and appeared at the train station in time to see the train departing. As the train pulled out, he ran alongside waving and yelling, "Karola! Karola!" She made her escape just in time!

※

Later in life, Karolina Grabiec thought that life and survival in West Virginia was nothing to brag about but must be remembered. I believe that we and generations to follow must know and appreciate the courageous determination, love, and faith that established the foundations of our heritage.

Even though she rarely spoke of him, Karolina expressed bitter feelings toward her husband Frank Sr. as the years went by. Now she was alone caring for eight children. But again, she remembered she was not alone.

Through it all Karolina felt the blessed sense of God's presence. She knew He did not bring her to America to leave her in poverty, but through the testing of her faith she developed perseverance (James 1:3). She always knew she could cast her anxiety on Him for He cared for her (1 Peter 5:7). This gave her irrepressible hope for the future.

She knew God was with her at every step of her life. He sustained her in every trial, day by day, moment by moment. She is with Him now and rejoicing that she kept her faith and did not waver or succumb to the pressures of this world.

As the years went by, Karolina was heartbroken as she wondered if she would ever see her first child Mañia again. But she was thankful for her parents, Mary and Joseph Franek, who cared for Mañia in Czechoslovakia, and trusted that God was with them.

Mañia with her Grandparents Mary Marcal and Joseph Franek

Part Three: A New Beginning

8

Chicago - Starting Over

We are afflicted in every way, but not crushed; perplexed, but not despairing; persecuted, but not forsaken; struck down, but not destroyed.
2 Corinthians 4:8-9 (NAS)

A **new way of life** was waiting for the Grabiecs in 1929. The train ride to Chicago seemed to last several days, Agnes remembers. But even if it wasn't that long it sure felt like it to her as a young girl. On the train, the generous passengers shared their meals with the five Grabiec children since they had left Galloway with little money. Annie, the youngest and only about four years old, loved to sing and dance in the aisles of the train doing the Charleston, kicking up her feet and laughing. She was quite a dancer, and the passengers loved it, Frank Jr. recalls. Agnes remembers eating sandwiches and watching people being served coffee in paper cups from the large coffeepot on a cart that was moved up and down the aisle. Unfortunately all five children got sick while on the train. But they were on a new adventure, and they all survived–again.

New Neighborhood for the Grabiec Children

The train arrived in Chicago at night. Their friend, Paul Lichner, Ann's husband, picked them up at the train depot in his Model-T Ford.

They were so excited to be riding around Chicago with him in his car. They were "google-eyed," as Frank Jr. describes it, looking at store windows, cars, clothes, lights, and busy streets for the first time. Agnes never forgot how, to her, it looking like a "dreamland at Christmas."

In contrast, Helen remembered a dangerously close call soon after arriving in Chicago when she was about nine. A stranger showed her a doll with eyes that he said would light up when he plugged it in. She started to go with him into an isolated construction site, but "something" stopped her. She remembered she had been taught not to go anywhere with a stranger. God protected her that day.

With the help of the Lichners' son, Al, who was a cook on the train running between Chicago and Galloway, Karolina got a job with the railroad company. With this new job, Karolina and her children could stay in Chicago and not have such a hard life.

Karolina's specialty was cleaning the luxury Pullman car used by presidents, senators, and people of great wealth. The company trusted her to clean the fancy fixtures and properly care for the luxurious velvet seats and draperies while the car was parked on a side track and readied for the next dignitary's use. At other times Karolina cleaned and mended headrests and seats on the other cars, but when the "special" car came in, Karolina was the only person allowed to clean it.

Karolina also worked at a local bakery. The owner told her to take home the leftover bakery goods for the family each day. Often she brought home doughnuts or breads, and one day, nine pies! These were wonderful treats for her children and their friends who shared vegetables and whatever extra provisions they had. Another treat in the winters was when Helen could make Jell-O by putting it out on the fire escape for it to set up in the cold. With what little they all had, they got together often and pooled their resources for the benefit of all.

Surviving the Great Depression from 1929 to 1941 was not easy. My mother was almost ten when the stock market crashed in 1929, as the Grabiecs were struggling to make new lives for themselves.

1929 Grabiec Family

In the move from Galloway to Chicago the Grabiecs lost the freedoms of the country, but now they had other opportunities as well as challenges. They first had to learn to speak differently. Frank Jr. remembers, "When we arrived in Chicago we were so dumb! We didn't know English very well; we said 'you'ns' for 'you'." Even though that was an acceptable dialect for the little coal-mining town in West Virginia at the time, it was not acceptable in the city. They did speak Polish fluently, but now they had to master English.

The love and sharing of Karolina's brother Rudy, and friends Paul and Ann Lichner, had helped them to get started, but soon they were looking for a home of their own.

The family first moved to a flat near West Division Street and Meade Avenue on the west side of Chicago. The younger Grabiec children were happy to move away from one of their "mean" cousins who thought they were just "dumb hillbillies." Now they felt more at home "in their element." They were on welfare and knew they would survive. They were welcomed by their new neighbors, and Frank Jr. remembers, as an eight-year-old boy, his mother's "old" thirty-year-old friends and neighbors visiting at their home often.

In 1929 Frank Jr. had to go to school barefoot one day and was sent home for shoes. But he had none. How could he go to school when he didn't have shoes? Being poor in an affluent neighborhood, he knew he was the most conspicuous child in his class.

Frank Jr. also never owned a toy in his life. He remembers the day he found a four-inch toy canoe. When he lost it in the yard, he searched for it for days. He also remembers the boy next door who had many toy cars. One day Frank Jr. managed to get the boy aggravated enough to make him throw his cars over the fence at Frank Jr. Now Frank Jr. had all the cars! But to his dismay the boy's mother soon came to get them, accusing Frank Jr. of stealing them.

One stormy day in 1931 young Frank Jr. waited with his family and friends for Karolina to come home from work while a blizzard was raging outside. It took her three days to get home in that severe winter storm. The younger children were so hungry that, when a grocery vendor unhitched his horses and wagon and gave them the rotting potatoes, they were grateful. Even then they shared with their neighbors and friends.

Their next move was to May Street across from a reception hall. Frank Jr. remembers how he snuck downstairs to three or four wedding receptions to eat. Even though he was conspicuous, he wasn't thrown out. Five million people were out of work, and they knew he was a little boy simply trying to survive.

"I remember when we lived on May Street," Frank Jr. recalls, "Ma took us to the Catholic Church to enroll us. I don't know the details, but we all came home because we 'didn't qualify.' She probably was told how much it would cost and knew she could never afford it. How that affected Mom, I can't imagine—to suffer for her kids another day in another way."

Soon the family moved to a third-floor flat at 1743 West Huron Street. Frank Jr. remembers the day he asked his mother if he could have the last egg. She told him "No" because she needed it to make dumplings for the whole family. In a response not entirely unusual for a young boy, he took the egg and dropped it from the window of their third-floor flat. He still remembers watching the egg fall between the tall buildings which were only about four feet apart. And no one had dumplings that night!

In 1933 Willie, the son of their family friend, Julius Nemeth, worked for the *Chicago Tribune* newspaper. For the 1933 World's Fair he got ten-year-old Joseph Grabiec to sell papers. The first day Joe earned less than fifty cents. Then his brother Frank Jr. was enlisted to sell, and then the whole neighborhood of eight to ten boys—"the Huron-Street Gang"—got involved. With twelve million people now out of work, they were thankful to find jobs.

"Before the papers arrived every evening we met at Lake Shore and had fun jumping off the rocks and the breakwater and swimming 'bare bottomed' in Lake Michigan next to Shedd Aquarium. Six days a week 'the boys from Huron Street' hustled the evening *Tribune*, working the crowd outside of the 12th Street gate next to the World's Fair, from the Field Museum and Shedd Aquarium to the streetcar, which was at least a quarter mile. We walked for hours and hours at night on the cold streets, selling papers for two cents each, working our butts off," as Frank Jr. describes it. For every ten cents' worth of papers they sold, they earned a three-cent profit. Often they had earned thirty cents by the end of the day.

"People were nice to talk to. We often met people from all over the world. We worked all night and usually checked in to Willie about midnight. We never thought about spending a penny, even though it was very late and we were hungry and tired. We were tempted to jump off the streetcar and join a few friends to get a 5¢ White Castle hamburger on Chicago Avenue and Milwaukee, but we knew our mother could buy bread and bologna at ten cents a pound and feed the whole family."

When they got home late at night, if Karolina was asleep, Joseph and Frank Jr. quietly put the money under her pillow, but she usually waited up for them.

Being determined, my mother wanted to sell papers also. During the first year of the World's Fair in 1933, Karolina had said, "No, Helen. That is a boy's job." But during the second year, 1934, she gave in to Helen's persistence.

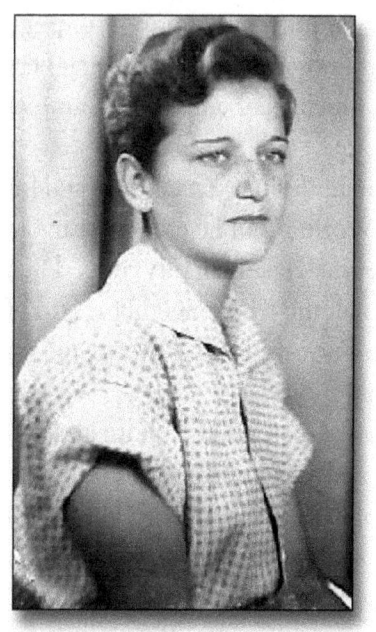
Young Helen

Helen occasionally outsold the boys, too, probably because of her beautiful smile when she got to do what she wanted!

Frank Jr. remembers somehow finding out about the free meals after school at the Union League Boys Club. He is still thankful today. "I had nothing, and somebody provided for me. I went there daily after school to eat, but first we had to take a teaspoonful of cod liver oil," Frank Jr. remembers. "It was a thick, hard-to-swallow, fishy, smelly glob. If you were hungry enough, you took it! Then we ate tuna or peanut butter sandwiches and drank Ovaltine. I never missed a meal."

Frank Jr. also remembers sneaking out the window of his third-floor flat to go to the Union League Boys Club to learn to swim and learn to use the wood shop, print shop, craft shop, and library. "We even got dental services there and radio technology classes at night," Frank Jr. recalls.

He will never forget the two-week camping experiences in Salem, Wisconsin. A wonderful lady named Mrs. Howe saw to it that he could go to camp for 50¢, even though the fee was $7. She also was the one who made sure the kids were dry after swimming before letting them go home on cold winter days.

Frank Jr. remembers that in the library he picked up a book on the elements of radio. He remembers reading it and thinking "I understand this!" He soon learned to make a crystal set–a "free radio!" Frank Jr.'s determined spirit would later help him to become an accomplished and renowned electronics technician.

"The rent for our flat on Huron Street was $18 a month," Frank Jr. remembers. "And welfare didn't pay poor people's rent. Evidently we didn't either, and one day when I returned home from my adventures in Chicago,

I didn't have a place to live! All our possessions were out in the street. They threw us out—we were 'street people.'

"My sister, Helen, and one other sister went looking for another house. I didn't have much hope for them. How could they convince a new landlord to let us move in? It was impossible, I thought. But, somehow they did it—God provided again. We moved into a better neighborhood at 1441 North Bell Avenue—two doors from my future sweetheart and wife, June Keck."

1326 Wicker Park Avenue was the last home for the Grabiecs as a family. They all continued to work hard so that all of them could survive, and some were able to continue their education.

The Depression had forced them to be ingenious in finding ways to survive. Besides learning to economize, work hard and not complain, Karolina taught all her children how to cook. Agnes remembers several of her restaurant jobs in Chicago. One chef had her do his cooking for him, including turkeys and roasts, even though he took the credit for the delicious meals! Agnes and all the Grabiecs became good cooks.

The family's frugality also helped them survive these difficult years. One motto Frank Jr. remembers was "Use it up, wear it out, make it do, or do without." It took ingenuity to do this, and the Grabiecs were good at it!

<hr>

Family unity and support were fostered by Karolina. It was vital for her to teach her children that, no matter what happened, they needed to stick together. When the children thought their mother was favoring one child over the others, she would put her ten fingers tightly together to symbolize the importance of all ten fingers to the well-being of the hands and to the whole body and say, "You think I love one better than the others? You are like my fingers. If you squeeze one, I feel it; and it hurts. You cannot separate one from the ten without feeling it." For the rest of their lives her children helped and supported each other. They survived the bad times and celebrated the good times. They each could count on the others without exception.

Karolina was strict in a quiet way. She did not know how much education her children would be able to get, but she knew that what *she* taught them would be valuable in their lives. The virtues she taught her children were honesty, reliability, family loyalty, faith and trust in God, and a sense of humor. She taught them to be obedient to His Ten Commandments and to the Golden Rule, "Do unto others as you would have them do unto you." She demonstrated kindness, sharing, love, a sense of peace, and satisfaction in hard work. With this foundation she knew they would also learn by doing, by experiencing life, by analyzing the results, and by learning from their mistakes. My mother remembered her mother saying, "If you make a mistake—recognize it, learn from it, admit it, and forget it."

Frank Jr. believes that the greatest blessing is to have something to give, and then to give it. He remembers when they had one chicken in the pot for the whole family to share. He also remembers when his mother had nothing to give. "What can I do for my kids?" she would lament. There were many times when she wanted to give to her children and couldn't. It was her torture and caused her great misery—having nothing to give to her children when she wanted to so desperately. Then she remembered to trust God. *"Co będzie, co będzie,"* she would say in Polish. "What will be, will be." And they survived another day.

But Frank Jr. will never forget going to grade school and high school hungry. He often had nothing to eat at lunch time. He saw others with large Pepsis and hot meals on their plates, and he walked around waiting for lunch to be over. But he had a brother and sisters in the same boat, and he didn't feel sorry for himself. He always felt close to them and knew that if *they* survived, he would also.

"Seeing how easy some of our children have it today," Frank Jr. ponders, "how will the next generation learn to survive?"

But *this* was Karolina's dream—that her children and grandchildren could become educated, have a better life, and *not* have to work so hard, just to survive.

9

Foundations and Friends

Suffering produces perseverance; perseverance, character; and character, hope. Romans 5:3b

Karolina had the ability to give her children a foundation of confidence and emotional security. "When things were really bad and I was cold or hungry and I went to her with my problems, I always left feeling comforted and reassured," Frank Jr. remembers. "She always built us up and never tore us down," Joe recalls. "Mom knew growth was necessary even though it could be uncomfortable. She described the discomfort of change and growth as "shaking the bag," Joe remembers.

Jobs and education in Chicago required the commitment and support of each member of the Grabiec family. With her determination, love, and faith Karolina taught all her children to be good and dependable workers. They found and kept jobs in Chicago at a time when jobs were scarce. Frances worked taking care of the youngest four Grabiec children, while Verna, Betty, and Agnes worked outside the home to help support the family. Betty was so lonesome working in homes away from her family that she was happy when she could work and baby-sit in the house next door. Agnes was happy, too, because she could go over to visit Betty after she got home from her restaurant job or factory work in the city.

In 1935 President Franklin Roosevelt promised "a chicken in every pot" and signed into law the Works Progress Administration (WPA), which provided work opportunities for the Grabiecs as well as for millions of people on relief.

1931 First Holy Communion

With Karolina and her four older daughters working, the younger four children were able to stay in school full time. The older four attended "continuation school" one day a week until age sixteen. Karolina's friend, Ann Lichner, gave Frank Jr. her son Al's compass, T-square, and other supplies while Frank and Joseph attended Crane Technical High School for boys from which they later graduated.

Karolina had wanted her children to go to Catholic schools, but because of the high fees they attended the public schools. Yet having raised her children in the Catholic faith Karolina proudly attended Agnes' and Helen's first Holy Communion at St. John's Church in Chicago.

As a teen, Helen worked in a beauty shop for a while. She was known for her skill in making stylish "finger waves." But she remembered a client whose hair she did not want to style. Frank Rossi's mother had asked Helen to finger-wave her son's hair because she did it so well. However, Mother refused because the boy had angered her with his flirtatious behavior. He had kissed her when she didn't want to be kissed. The neighbor pleaded with Karolina to make Helen wave his hair, so she did, but only as a favor to her mother.

Joseph, as a teenager, enjoyed his new job as a messenger for Postal

Helen with Frank Rossi

Telegraph. "I delivered messages even in the freezing cold and pouring rain," he remembers. His uniform looked so much like a police uniform that some people thought he was a police officer. Some would not even open the door for him, he recalls, and he had to slip their messages under the door. One good result of looking like a police officer was that his bike was never stolen!

Joseph as Postal Messenger

While in grade school and high school, Frank Jr. remembers how my mother Helen wrote interesting stories about her life and adventures as a coal-miner's daughter in West Virginia. She also wrote numerous letters to friends and family members as they grew up, traveled, and moved across the country.

Helen was a serious student and was intelligent as well as beautiful. She was shy, though, and her personality was kept pretty much hidden until late in her senior year of high school. When she joined the swim team she started to be more expressive. She blossomed in math class and became more outspoken and witty.

Mom loved her years in school. All her life she kept her swim team pin, pep club pin, and her 1934 autograph book[11] from Talcott School. She also attended Burr Elementary School and Wells High School, which opened in 1935. Helen got good grades and was the first Grabiec in the family to graduate from high school. This was only possible by the hard work and unity of the family, pulling together and supporting one another.

1937 Helen in High School

Agnes remembers Helen's graduation day, reminiscing, "Helen was one of the smartest children. She went to school every day; she learned what she had to learn. When I went to see her graduate, I was

Ann, Helen, Agnes, Betty, Frances, and Verna

so proud of her. She had the name of Wells High School on her sweater, and I'll never forget her singing the graduation song!" After hearing her beautiful voice singing the graduation song, one of Helen's teachers expressed irritation at her for not having joined the school choir. "Helen, why were you so shy these past years in high school? You're smarter than you let on!" Helen was surprised at the question and realized, then, that she could have enjoyed high school even more if she had not been so reserved.

Joseph, Karolina, and Frank Jr.

Perhaps her shyness had developed from being an immigrant's daughter, being brought up in a small town, having to learn English as a second language, and being called a D.P. ("displaced person"). She and her brothers and sisters had been teased and felt all the ramifications of being immigrant children in the big city.

In 1935, with the help of her eighteen-year-old daughter, Betty, Karolina, at age forty-two, filled out a four-page citizenship application, entitled "Application for a Certificate of Arrival and Preliminary Form for a Declaration of Intention." The papers were never finalized, however. Perhaps this was because of the expense of the filing fee, or because Karolina would not have been able to pass the English speaking, reading, and writing test.

Friendships and fun during difficult years fostered lifelong relationships and memories for the Grabiecs. Karolina had come to America with several family friends, one of whom was Julius Nemeth who became the owner of a barber shop in Chicago. His son, William (we called him "Willie"), became a good friend of Karolina and all her children and grandchildren. The love, confidence, optimism, and energy shown by the family of six sisters and two brothers and their mother attracted many friends to the Grabiec family over the years.

Frank Jr. with Landlord

Even the old Polish landlord of their flat on Wicker Park became a good friend to the family, as seen in the photograph. Grandmother Karolina took many photos of her young-adult children and their friends in Chicago.

For relaxation and entertainment the family and friends got together often to sing, laugh and talk, take walks, sit on the front steps of their flat, and just enjoy each other's company.

Frank Jr. still remembers his good friend, Chester Pokrzywa. The two of them encouraged each other in the study of electronics. "Chester was one step ahead of me," Frank Jr. reminisces. "He sent out codes with his amateur radio using his call letters W9-IOI." Sadly, Chester was killed serving in World War II in the Philippines, Frank Jr. learned later.

Another good friend was Mike Cernuska who worked in a bakery and often brought pastries and baked goods for the family and friends to share. Mike served in the U. S. Army and Mother described him as "a real human being." Mike was like part of the family, and when Mike's parents died, he and the Grabiecs continued looking after each other.

During these Depression years the Grabiecs found moments of joy in the dancing and singing that was part of their lives. Their Uncle Rudy played the flute and the clarinet ("licorice stick" as they called it) in a tavern on Division Street and other local taverns. The families and friends danced or sat and enjoyed the music.

For fun some of the Grabiecs and their friends often walked to Lake Michigan to the beach. They walked to the Navy pier and swam on warm days. Agnes went in too far one day, she recalls, and her friend grabbed her and pulled her out, saving her from drowning.

Another special time for family and friends was packing a lunch and going to town to watch five-cent movies all day, as well as a stage show. Cousin Carole Jane remembers even at a young age she was able to go downtown with no worries of danger. Cousin Audrey loved going to the Aragon Ballroom to enjoy the music and watch people dance. She also remembers my mother taking her to visit their good friend Willie at work at the Chicago Tribune.

One of Helen's favorite pastimes was her voice lessons with the premier coloratura soprano, Rosalinda Morini, of the Chicago Civic Opera Company. Mother had a beautiful voice. Her singing was her passion, and she continued to sing all of her life.

Besides sewing, crocheting was a favorite pastime for Karolina. For the winter she crocheted beautiful sweaters for her children, and they often shared their warm clothes with each other. Joseph will never forget the day he let Helen borrow his sweater. When he wore it the next day, his friends asked him why he had two bumps on the front of his sweater. I don't think he let her borrow it from then on!

10

Karolina's Spirit in Her Nine Children

Live in harmony with one another, be sympathetic, love as brothers, be compassionate and humble. 1 Peter 3:8

Karolina's spirit of determination, love, and faith lived and continued to live on in each of her nine children. The Grabiec family was happy in helping one another and knew the joy of giving. They also experienced the satisfaction of being needed by those around them. Instead of trying to outdo each other, they supported the efforts of family, friends, and neighbors. They laughed together, and they cried together. They worked and played together. They shared the good times as well as the bad times. It was the way Karolina had raised them; it's what seemed natural to them.

Verna, one of Karolina's twin daughters, learned much while working in the early '30s as a nanny for Dr. Winestock and his family in Chicago. She loved fashion and flower arranging and became very business minded. She became renowned for her creative millinery skills, designing fashionable hats and glamorous wedding veils. She was also known for making the best *pierogi* (fried filled rolls), poppy-seed coffee cakes, and designer wedding cakes.

Verna married Joesph Kropp in Chicago on March 26, 1935, and they moved to a bungalow two and one-half blocks from her mother, Karolina. Verna had a beautiful coloratura soprano voice. Helen had suggested that Verna go with her to sing in New York, but her husband did not agree with the idea. Verna was heartbroken.

Their first daughter, Audrey Ann, was born on January 20, 1936, one of the coldest days on record in Chicago. Karolina wanted to be with Verna in the hospital since she was having a very long labor. While waiting for a streetcar Karolina got chilled and developed pneumonia. This was the second blow to Karolina's delicate lungs. Not only did she suffer from the coal dust from the mines, but now she had pneumonia and asthma.

On January 13, 1941, Verna and Joe's second daughter, Betty Jo, was born. Their third daughter, Frances Laura, was born on March 24, 1944. Their son, Joseph, completed their family on January 11, 1945.

After her family moved to Phoenix, Verna was active in her church, helping out with Bible School classes and church plays. She took college classes, loved painting and drawing, and wrote sensitive poetry.[12]

Verna and Joe Kropp

I remember Aunt Verna as an expressive and delightful person to be around. She was strict with us kids, but she always was caring and had a good sense of humor.

Aunt Verna was always kind to me. Once when I was in the hospital for surgery at age twenty-one, she bought me a beautiful matching nightgown and robe. I was touched by her thoughtfulness. I also remember going to visit her one New Year's Eve when I was in her neighborhood. It was fun just sitting around, all dressed up, snacking and talking throughout the evening.

Many years after her husband had died, Verna sang in a Polish choir in Phoenix. When she started dating a man in the choir, I asked her, "Are you going to marry him?"

"No," she said, "If I do, he will stop treating me like a queen!"

Frances, Verna's twin, was beloved by the children in all the Grabiec families. They knew her as strict yet loving, and they felt secure being with her. Frances was also a good cook. Her *golabki* (stuffed cabbage rolls) were the best! As a skilled seamstress she designed beautiful clothes for family members as well as professionally. I loved the large-collared dress she made for me when I was young.

Frances was a sensitive person whose dreams often came true. Her canary died right after she dreamed that an owl came into the house and killed it. In another dream she knew when one of the men in the family (my Dad) was wounded during the war.

Frances met Silas Meardy in 1933 while working as a waitress in Chicago. She was wearing a beautiful sweater that Karolina had crocheted for her. Noticing the sweater and her bustiness, he commented, "You are a little top-heavy, Toots." And looking at her name tag, he asked, "What is the other one named?" Watching him staring at her, Frances retorted, "That's not on the menu!" She was so embarrassed she never wore that sweater again. They married two weeks later.

Karolina's first grandchild, Carole Jane, was born to Frances and Si on November 27, 1935. Karolina's first grandson, Richard Eugene, was born on April 20, 1939.

Frank Jr. remembers meeting Silas when Frank was young and naïve in Chicago. Frank was impressed with Silas as a smart and successful businessman, owning a twelve-chair barber shop.

The Meardy Family

Si became not only Frank's brother-in-law but also a wonderful friend and father figure to him.

Frank Jr. has fond memories of hunting and fishing trips with Silas in the Mackinaw River in Green Valley and in other lakes and rivers. Si let Frank Jr.

drive his car and in the summers invited him to stay with him and Frances in Green Valley, Bartonville, or Peoria—wherever they were living in Illinois at the time. Frank Jr. credits these experiences, as well as numerous conversations with Si, as having helped him develop in his formative teen and young adult years.

Years later, to honor the memory of Si, Frank Jr. commissioned an architect-designed bell tower to be built at the YMCA Sky-Y Camp in Prescott, Arizona, to house a bell donated by Frances. Frank Jr. remembered how he loved ringing the school bell as a child in West Virginia. Now, years later, kids love to ring the Sky-Y Camp bell that Frank Jr. had installed as a lasting memorial to the man who meant so much to him.

I remember visiting Aunt Frances and Uncle Si's home and their barber shop next door. He had huge barber chairs we liked to sit in, and he gave us peppermint sticks and pop. Having never lived on a farm, I was fascinated that their milk came in large milk jugs with the cream on top. And I remember that the men played penny ante and other poker games in the basement every night.

Frances always empathized with the children. She was sensitive to the changes in them as they were influenced by others and the world. When my son, Zac, was born, she said, "Bring him over today so I can see him before he takes on anyone else's personality." She knew babies learned fast from their environment.

Betty, as a girl, was quiet and serious at times and loved to read. Yet to Frank Jr., "She was the most outgoing of all my sisters. She was a very devoted Catholic and always kept me in her prayers. She was the hub of the family wheel, always maintained communication, and seemed to inherit Karolina's motherly spirit. She also kept in touch with her Galloway friends. She had a great sense of humor and loved to clown around.

Betty met Carl Bulanda at the wedding of Carl's brother Joe to Betty's good friend Tillie. They fell in love, he proposed after three days, and they were married six months later in Cleveland, Ohio, on October 26, 1935. Carl had only one week's pay, but he insisted that Betty quit her $28-a-week job at the picture-frame factory. When they moved to Cleveland to begin their life together, Carl made $13 a week and life was tough. They lived upstairs in his parents' home for a while. Betty could not afford a 25¢ broom and swept the floor with rags until her sister-in-law, Jean, bought her a broom.

Betty and Carl's son, James Edward, was born on July 20, 1944, and their daughter, Marilyn Elizabeth, was born on July 22, 1947.

I remember Aunt Betty's beautiful home and gardens in Bedford, Ohio. I'll never forget the day Aunt Betty took us to church—whoever wanted to go. I went with her, and it was my first experience in a Catholic church. I am inspired and proud of her as I think back on the experience. She loved God, and because she was a positive influence on me, I want to be that to the children in my family.

Betty and Carl Bulanda

Before Carl died, he made sure Betty learned to drive a car. He wanted her to be able to be independent if anything should happen to him. Thus she became the only one of the seven Grabiec sisters to learn to drive a car.

Agnes' love and life with Otto Berndt is truly a unique one. How could they know their love and lives together would last over sixty-three years—the longest in the family?

They met one day when Agnes was coming home from work. Otto was leaning on a fence at his mother's home, which was across the street from Agnes' family's third floor flat.

He asked, "Hey, what're you goin' to do, little 'Polak'?"

"I'm goin' to do whatever I want," she replied. "Nothin' special."

He asked her to go downtown to see a show, and she said, "OK." The show was *Going My Way,* with Bing Crosby, Agnes remembers.

Agnes decided Otto was the one for her. They married on August 2, 1941 in Chicago. Their first son, Earl William, was born on July 8, 1942, while

Otto and Agnes Berndt

Otto was far away, fighting for freedom in Europe during World War II. Otto did not see his firstborn son until he returned from the war when Earl was almost three years old. Their second son, Leslie Steven, was born on August 7, 1950. After much prayer to God, Linda Susan was born on September 16, 1958, fulfilling Agnes' desire for a daughter to bless her life.

Later in life, Earl served in the U. S. Navy, and Leslie served in the U. S. Army. Sadly, Leslie died in 1992 at the young age of forty-two. Agnes and Otto recently celebrated their 63rd wedding anniversary. Both in their late eighties, Agnes and Otto still tease each other and banter[13] back and forth, saying,

"Do you still love me?"

"Yes, for now I do, anyway."

"Well, I still love you, too."

Agnes and Otto are truly a remarkable couple. Agnes enjoys having company and likes to talk about her love for Otto and for her mother Karolina. She was close to my mom and shares with me much about their lives growing up in Galloway and Chicago. She still remembers the old coal miner's song from living in Galloway. She laughs, cries, talks, and shows me her old photos as well as the new photos of her kids, grandkids, and great-granddaughter.

Agnes is lively, generous, and a good cook (especially her delicious nut roll). For years she remembered the birthdays and anniversaries of all her loved ones. On one of my visits recently she said, "I wish someone would make some doughnuts like my mother used to make." Well, I remember how my mother, her sister Helen, used to make them, but recently I used a recipe in a cookbook. They were good, but different. I told Aunt Agnes that next time I would make them like their mother did—with the raised roll dough recipe. But they will still "not be the same" because Grandma Karolina won't be making them.

Aunt Agnes makes me remember to appreciate the important things in life—God, our families, our freedoms, and the blessings of living in America. These are extremely important to her. Her husband, Otto, and my dad, James, were two of millions who gave up years of their young adult lives during World War II. She scolded me when I bought a foreign-made car as a young adult. "Why did you buy that car—it was not made in America!" she admonished. I could see the seriousness in her face and never forgot it! Many in her generation do not take it lightly when we support a country which had been our enemy during the war years.

Frank is a generous man who has always shared what he has with family and friends. In 1942 Frank joined the United States Marine Corps and served three and one-half years, receiving the rank of staff sergeant as an electronics technician. His only war injury was that he got malaria in Guadalcanal—the victim of a mosquito bite.

Frank married his "war bride," June Keck, May 1, 1944, in Chicago and later moved to Phoenix. Their first son, Wayne Carl, was born December 14, 1946. Their daughter, Carolyn Lee, was born October 5, 1949, and was named after Karolina. Gary Steven, their second son, was born December 7, 1953.

June and Frank Grabiec Jr.

In gratitude for his experiences with the Union League Boys Club in Chicago, Frank has given of his time and resources for many years to the YMCA in Phoenix. In their appreciation of his service, they have erected a second bell tower in his honor at their YMCA Chauncy Ranch Camp.

Over the years, Frank and June hosted many family gatherings at their home during holidays, special occasions, and just for fun. There was always lots of food—with everyone bringing "pot luck" and his sisters and brother pitching in. He also took the time to organize family reunions at the YMCA camps.

Frank believes the Grabiecs never had a lack of security in their lives. "We never felt sorry for ourselves," he reminisces. "But we could not do it alone; we needed each other." He knew that one can do the work of one; two can do the work of three; three can do the work of five, and so on. He knew that a cord of three strands is not quickly broken (Ecclesiastes 4:12b).

"If my family survived while I was surviving, it was all right," he said. "Now I'm over-blessed!" he stressed as he glanced at all the electronics equipment in his shop, Dyna Tronics, which he founded in 1952 in Phoenix. "But it's still more fun fixing that old radio up there in the corner," he said, pointing to the shelf of recycled electronics.

Uncle Frank is quite the character. He amazes us with his never-ending endurance. He learned the electronics business from the bottom up and is a self-educated electronics engineer. Take any old favorite radio, TV, microwave, or sound system to him, and he can fix it! He may have to look far and wide for the parts, but when he finds them, he stocks up. He even makes the parts if he has to. In his shop you will also find old reconditioned units for sale, thus recycling in a unique way. Frank has been honored as president of the International Society of Certified Electronic Technicians and also as president of the Arizona State Electronics Association. In August 1997 Frank Grabiec was inducted into the Electronics Hall of Fame "for outstanding service to mankind through contributions to the advancement of the electronics industry."

If you get a chance to talk to him, you will also enjoy Frank's great sense of humor and wit. He reminds me so much of my mother, his closest sister in age. I'm sure the two of them had a blast all their lives, talking and laughing about life and being optimistic through it all. They always saw the glass as "half full!" They also were optimistic about it being refilled when it was empty, such as when I had broken something, and Uncle Frank did not worry about it. He said, "Everything is meant to be consumed."

Joseph moved to Phoenix in 1944. He and Matreena married on

October 18, 1948, and they have four beautiful daughters. Marlene Susan was born on October 18, 1952; Kathleen Joyce was born March 18, 1955; Diana Kay was born March 8, 1959; and Denise Lavonne was born on September 3, 1961.

With his quick smile and a positive attitude, Uncle Joe makes me laugh. When I was a child and told him something, he teased me by saying, "You're just saying that 'cause it's true." When I wanted to do something, he always said, "OK!" even if we didn't do it.

As a teenager I stayed with Uncle Joe and Aunt Matreena to help care for their two babies while he recovered from surgery and Matreena worked outside of the home. I enjoyed staying with them and remember waking up to the radio every morning. One unforgettable experience was when Aunt Matreena and I had fun making delicious divinity candy one day, and I ate so much I got sick!

Joseph and Matreena Grabiec

Joe is "the angel of the family," his brother Frank calls him. He has been a strong and gentle supporter of all the family. For many years he took care of his mother, Karolina, in Phoenix. More recently he took care of his sister Frances until she died. He also drove Frank to and from work, church, and home following heart surgery, and recently cared for a dying nephew.

Joe has done much to help in his community also. For years he walked his neighborhood with a block watch to deter drugs and crime. Uncle Joe is optimistic and always finds a reason to be thankful. Even when my dad died on August 24, 1977, Joe considered it an honor that Dad died on his birthday.

Uncle Joe is always there for us. We will never be able to repay him, but I know God has great rewards for all those unseen acts of kindness and goodness he has done for family, friends, neighbors, and the community as a whole. "Your Father, who sees what is done in secret, will reward you" (Matthew 6:6b).

Annie was my mother's youngest sister and the "baby" of the Grabiec family. She was the "charmer," and she looked like a doll. My sisters and I have bought several dolls that remind us of her beauty.

While in Chicago, Annie married Elmer Gewelke on January 1, 1942. For a time they lived on Meade Avenue, Elmer recalls. In 1943 they came to visit Karolina in Phoenix for a month. Their first son, Donald Barry, was born on June 22, 1946. Their second son, Douglas Steven, was born August 2, 1949. In 1951 they moved to Phoenix, and Cynthia Joy, their first daughter, was born on May 5, 1956. Two years later,

Annie and Elmer Gewelke

their second daughter, Laura Jean, was born on April 29, 1958. My mother always thought that Laura's beautiful hair was like Karolina's—auburn, thick and long.

Annie had a beautiful smile, and took much pride in her appearance. She had a lilting soprano voice and sang in the church choir. Annie and Elmer always had a neat and stylish home. Annie was a good cook, and they loved the family get-togethers.

Kleofas' and Mañia's Wedding Photo (date unknown)

In 1966 the Grabiecs finally got to meet their eldest sister Mañia Grabiec Bielczykova—the child Karolina had to leave behind in Czechoslovakia in 1913.

"Mañia, where are you going?" her neighbor in Czechoslovakia asked, as she peeked through her shutters and saw Mañia walking down the street with her suitcase.

"I'm going to America!" she called up to her neighbor's apartment window.

"Liar!" her neighbor retorted. Even though she had told her neighbors that some day she was going to America, they did not believe her.

Mañia had her mother's determined spirit, however, and always had faith that she would meet her sisters and brothers some day. Karolina died in 1955 having never seen her first-born daughter again after leaving Czechoslovakia. But now Helen and her five sisters and two brothers had contributed enough money to bring Mañia to the United States. They were going to meet their sister for the first time. Frances, Betty, and Betty's husband Carl wrote letters, organized the trip, collected the money, sent it to Czechoslovakia, and then they waited. It took a long time for the tickets and visa to be processed. At that time, Mañia's husband, Kleofas Bielczyk, was not allowed to leave the country to ensure Mañia's return.

1947 Mañia and Kleofas Bielczyk

At age fifty-six, Mañia received her six-month visa, boarded the plane, and flew to New York City. Seeing her for the very first time, Betty and Frances thought she looked just like their mother. Betty, Frances, and Verna remembered much of their Polish language so were able to talk with her and interpret for the family.

When they arrived at the train depot in Phoenix, all nine sisters and brothers were together for the very first time.

"They didn't believe me!" Mañia exclaimed as she described her Czechoslovakian neighbors' reaction. "I told them I was going to go to America to meet my sisters and brothers. They said it would never happen, but I made it! I'm here!" Frank Jr. thought it would be a great idea to ask a news reporter to write an article about this unique story. Mañia expressed her fears, however, that the news could be unfavorable to her country and cause her problems back home.

Family members took Mañia on a six-month journey around the United

1966 Mañia Meets Her Sisters and Brothers
Betty, Frances, Helen, Mañia, Joe, Agnes, Frank Jr.,
Annie, Verna

States visiting the rest of the family, and she liked the United States very much. She thought the people of America were warm and friendly, and she cried the first time she went into a grocery store filled with foods of all kinds. She commented that, in Czechoslovakia (at that time), oranges were only available during the Christmas season. She was also surprised that groceries were bagged for you in disposable paper bags; back home she had to bring her own shopping bag.

Even though I owned a seven-year-old '59 Oldsmobile at the time, Aunt Mañia told me I was "rich" and that very few people owned cars in Karvina. Also, most people were not allowed to buy houses. She and her husband had always lived in an apartment.

It was fun for me to watch Mañia and my younger brother, John, communicate. He was about ten at the time, and even though hey did not know each other's language, they communicated pretty well with expressions, hand motions, and body language.

Mañia told us some of what had happened to her while growing up in

Czechoslovakia. She was not allowed to go to school as she wished but was told she would crochet and sew in the textile industry. Some of the things she made were dresses, sweaters, coats, scarves, hats, slippers, socks, curtains, table cloths, dolls, and doll clothes. She brought beautiful crocheted gifts for everyone, and we could appreciate her talents. Like Karolina's, Mañia's hands were never idle. She always had her knitting or crocheting needles handy—fingers flying while she talked.

During Mañia's visit in America, her sisters and brothers shared with her that years earlier their mother had sent money for her to come and join them in America. Mañia said she never got it but had received lard instead. She told them that the second time they sent money, she did receive it but at that time she did not want to leave the grandparents who had raised her.

When Mañia visited Karolina's gravesite, she was so moved that she wept and said she wanted to dig through to the casket to see her mother and hug her. Her sisters and brothers were shocked at this. Only then did they realized how

Together at Karolina's Gravesite

desperately Mañia had wanted to know her mother.

In preparing to leave after her first visit, Mañia lined her suitcases with foil and packed razor blades and other items to take back to Czechoslovakia. Upon arrival, the authorities confiscated most of her items and kept her for several days trying to determine why she would do that.

When she got home and told her husband, Kleofas, and her friends about her six-month visit to America, they couldn't believe all she had to say. They disbelieved the life we take for granted!

On her second and final visit in 1976, Mañia brought her husband to experience the United States for himself. The family took him all over the country, including the Grand Canyon and Las Vegas, Nevada. He also loved it. We asked them if they would consider moving here. Mañia told us that even though Kleofas had been told he could receive his pension here, they could not be sure that he would.

As Mañia and Kleofas were preparing to return to Czechoslovakia, her sisters and brothers asked her if they could mail gifts of clothes or coats to her. She told them to send wrinkled material and blankets which were less likely to be confiscated, and she would use them to make her clothes and winter coats.

In the 1980s Frances, Betty, and Betty's husband Carl visited Mañia in Czechoslovakia. At the time they were there, however, Mañia found it difficult to find enough food to feed them. She even tried to bribe the butcher to sell her the extra meat she needed.

In 1997 Frances' granddaughter, Karyn, also went to visit Mañia. To communicate they spoke German, a language they both knew. From then on the family kept in touch with long-distance phone calls as well as cards and letters.

"Beyond the Sunset" was one of the Grabiec family's favorite songs, and the sun was beginning to set for some in the family. On May 12, 1986, Annie was the first of the Grabiec children to pass into eternity. Even though she had been ill for many years, she achieved one of her last wishes which was to live at least to age sixty-two, as her dear mother had done. After long and full lives, Betty died on April 13, 1994, at age seventy-nine, and Frances died on

March 7, 1998, at age eighty-four. Before Christmas of 2000 Mom asked me to send Mañia a Christmas card, but after several months the card was returned to us marked *"Décédé"* (deceased). We knew then that she had died, at or near the age of ninety, joining her mother, father, and three of her sisters in the bliss of eternity, young and beautiful again.

The Grabiec family's ability to thrive in times of struggle is an inspiration to me. The fruit of the Spirit of God that lived in their mother also blossomed in them. Their foundation of faith gave them the peace, security, and optimism to count their daily blessings as they continued to work hard for their future.

Even today my aunts and uncles who are still with us are, and always have been, so appreciative of small daily blessings. They appreciate each other and are kind to all they meet. They rarely get angry and are very forgiving. There is no way I could list all they have done to help family and friends through all the years. They are in their eighties and nineties now and still sharing their wisdom and helping in any way they can.

They will still bear fruit in old age. Psalm 92:14a

11

West to Arizona

He guided them to their desired haven.
Psalm 107:30b

Six months to live" was what Dr. Tobotnick had given Karolina in 1938 if she stayed in Chicago. Her asthma was becoming worse and he recommended a drier climate. Helen, who was very close to her mother, knew she had to get Karolina out of the damp, coal-burning air as quickly as possible. She had heard of Arizona's clear dry air which held the promise of improved health for her mother.

The Grabiecs' long-time family friend, Willie Nemeth, knew Karolina and her family had no money for train fare but told her of a possible ride to the West. He knew that two cars were going to be driven from Detroit to the west coast, and a friend of his was going to drive one of the cars. His friend offered to let Karolina, her nineteen-year-old daughter, Helen, and fourteen-year-old daughter, Annie,

Karolina and Helen in Chicago

ride along as passengers for the long trip. So with courage, determination, and faith they agreed. They planned to go to Arizona and stay in either Phoenix or Tucson.

Frank Jr. remembers the night his mother and two sisters left their home on Wicker Park Avenue in Chicago with a total of $12. "They just climbed into the car and disappeared into the night with no luggage, and going 'nowhere,'" as Frank Jr. describes the scene. They had no relatives to receive them and no promise of a job. All they knew was that they had to go to a drier climate to save Karolina's life. They did have faith, however, which can only be exercised in the unknown and unseen future.

Old Route 66 was the road west in 1938. After arriving in Phoenix, they decided to stay and rented a small house on Godfrey Street. Karolina, Helen, and Annie liked Phoenix very much, and Karolina felt much better there.

After a few months, however, they missed their family and friends in Chicago. Over the next ten years they made many trips by train back to Chicago and returned to Phoenix for the winters. On one trip to Phoenix Helen brought with her the twelve-year-old son of Rosalinda Morini, her friend and voice teacher. He, too, suffered with asthma in Chicago. He liked my mother and made her a tile-topped table which we still have today.

In Phoenix, Helen worked as a waitress at the San Carlos Hotel (which is still in existence). While she was working late one night, her boss asked her if she would mind waiting on one more customer even though it was closing time. She did, cheerfully of course as was her nature, and cattle rancher Mr. Tovrea left her a $100 tip!

James Alfred Hayden, born in Pauls Valley, Oklahoma, on October 21, 1918, also worked at the San Carlos Hotel. He worked as a bartender, desk clerk, and bell hop. James soon spotted the beautiful waitress, Helen Grabiec, and she was to become his "ray of sunshine."

1941 James (left) and a Friend in the U. S. Army

They wrote many letters to each other over the eight years while dating and while he was in the U. S. Army. The song "You Are My Sunshine" became "their song," and "Have I told You Lately That I Love You" became another one of their favorites.

On January 6, 1941, at age twenty-two James volunteered for what he thought was to be one year of service in the United States Army. Over the next nine months he wrote to Helen from training camps in Louisiana, Oklahoma, and Texas, as well as from other states. On September 25 he wrote to Helen from Camp Barkeley, Texas, asking her to join him on his next furlough in Chickasha, Oklahoma, to meet his family. When she did, his family immediately fell in love with her. (When his sister Madge wanted to inspect Helen's beautiful teeth, however, Helen felt like she was a horse at auction!)

Karolina, James, and Helen, May 18, 1941

Helen and James married in Chickasha, Oklahoma, on October 17, 1941. James (now usually called Jim) gave her a Cracker Jack ring with the promise of a diamond later. An informal wedding photo was taken, but they could not afford to buy it. A few months later Jim's father, Herbert, saw the photo in the window of the local pawn shop and bought it for them.

On November 8 Jim applied for a "dependant discharge" because he was now married. On November 13 his request was denied. Instead, his service was extended for eighteen more months. Then, when he was seventeen days from being discharged, the United States entered World War II after the December 7, 1941, attack on Pearl Harbor.

On December 30 Jim was sent to Camp Chorrera in the Panama Canal Zone for ten months. A severe spider bite put him in the hospital and left a quarter-size scar on his right hand. On November 9, 1942, he was sent back to the U. S. for twenty-two months of intensive training.

On one of his furloughs Helen brought Jim to Chicago to meet more of her family members. Agnes remembers meeting him before he left for the war. She told me, "Your dad danced with me at Wicker Park in Chicago!"

Cousin Audrey also remembers meeting my dad for the first time. "He was tall, handsome, and spoke with a smooth southern drawl." Mother's brother Joe asked her, "Why did you want to marry that string bean?"

"Because I love him," was her answer.

With Jim now moving all over the country in the service, Helen and her sister Annie continued to live with their mother in Phoenix. In 1949 their brother Joseph sold his car for $550 and sent it to Karolina to help pay the $1,750 for her little home at 1117 E. Mohave. Her home had a small living room, a kitchen, one bedroom, and one small bathroom. Later Joe cut down the tall, dusty, asthma-causing tamarack trees in her yard and pulled out the stumps. He also constructed her driveway and curbs. After he married, he built his home next door to hers and helped care for her the rest of her life.

Helen and Jim

Annie and Helen helped build a chicken coop, and with Jim coming home soon on furlough, they converted the shed in back of Karolina's house into a small apartment. While Jim was away during the war years, Helen decided to do what she had always wanted to do, which was to continue her singing career. When Jim arrived on furlough, he asked, "Why do we have a piano but no ice box?" Helen answered, cheerfully, "We can put food in my mother's ice box, but I need a piano to rehearse!"

War times were significant for those with a spirit of love for America, love for family, and self-confidence in having hope for the future. After the bombing of Pearl Harbor, cousin Audrey remembers hearing the voice of President Roosevelt announcing on the radio, ". . . a date which will live in infamy . . . ." She was five years old.

Helen and Jim

"Over the next few years, Victory Gardens were planted and we were so united," Audrey remembers. "If the family had too many tomatoes, or anything, they shared with their neighbors. Eventually there were many cars parked on the street with no tires. The rubber had been collected for the war effort as well as everyone's lard and grease for ammunition."

Those who left the security of their homes to fight in foreign lands had a spirit of gratitude and were willing to sacrifice their lives for their God-given freedoms—for the free enterprise system, for their freedom of worship, freedom of expression, freedom to persist in working hard to better their lives, and the freedom to continue their education as much or as little as they wanted.

During war times the Grabiecs supported the war effort, their friends and neighbors, and each other in any way they could. There were many jobs for them to do. Since many of the men were leaving for war, Helen worked running a chucker, spinning and cutting metal rods. Verna worked four to five hours a day and did piece work for the war tanks while Karolina took care of Verna's daughter, Audrey Anne.

Nancy Lee, Helen and Jim's first child, was born August 23, 1943, in Chicago. On September 20, 1944, with little Nancy only one year old and Helen expecting daughter number two, James was sent to fight in Europe.

On December 16, 1944, the Battle of the Bulge,[14] the biggest and bloodiest battle of World War II, began in northern France. Jim was there in the thick of it as a sergeant and medium tank commander with the 43rd Tank Battalion, 12th Armored Division, Seventh Army. On January 15, greatly outnumbered, he radioed the commanding officer for permission to retreat but was refused. Thirteen of his friends were killed that day.

"One of our men has been wounded, but I don't know which one!" Helen's sister Frances exclaimed one night, waking up suddenly and sitting bolt upright in bed. Frances often had dreams that came true. She called Helen in Phoenix and later found out the wounded man was Jim.

Wounded on January 15, 1945, Jim almost died from life-threatening injuries. He later told Helen's brother, Joe, about his out-of-body experience. He saw himself lying on top of another tank and saw the medic working hard to save his life. As he watched the medic jabbing his arm, trying to find a vein that wasn't collapsed, he thought "Why is he working so hard to save that man? He's dead." But, he survived.

Later, in the hospital, his left arm was amputated because his elbow had been blown off by a German 88. His leg was shattered in nine places from his ankle to his knee, and zinc plates were used to hold it together. Years later, the bone knitted so well to the plates that the doctors decided not to remove them. After thirty blood transfusions and having his spleen removed, James lived to face one of the greatest challenges of his life as a disabled veteran.

Since war mail was opened and censored for security purposes, Dad's letters described his hospital location as being "near the city with the same name as our daughter's," which was Nancy, France. Before he told Mom or the rest of his family what had happened, he tried to remain upbeat in his letters, but his mother knew by his shaky writing that something was wrong.

I was born on March 9, 1945, in Phoenix and was named after my father. When Grandmother Karolina saw me, she told my mother, "Helen, that's not your baby. She's an Indian papoose!" I had beautiful thick black hair and large eyes. On another day Mother was holding me while shopping, and when I moved

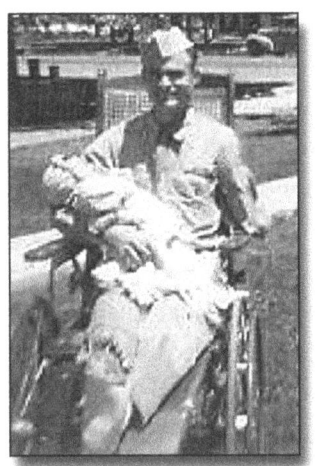

1945 Dad Holding Me in Utah

suddenly, the lady standing next to us jumped and exclaimed, "I thought you were holding a doll!"

During the war, loved ones were separated and then there was the joyous coming together again for some. On March 18, nine days after I was born, Dad arrived back in the United States having spent two months in a hospital in France. He and Mom could hardly wait to be reunited. On April 26, Dad wrote to Mom from Bushnell Hospital in Brigham City, Utah. He was glad that she was thinking about coming to be with him.

When I was two months old, Mother asked her sister Frances to keep nineteen-month-old Nancy with her at her home on Fayette Street in Peoria, Illinois, so Mom could go be with Dad. On May 13 Mom and I arrived in Utah. Mom was still nursing me at the time. One of his buddies said, "I wish *my* wife could be here and nurse our baby in front of me!"

"The winter in Utah was very cold," Mom said. "It was so cold we slept with our clothes on! We shared an apartment with a Mormon family, and in the morning, after everyone else had left, the lady of the house brought out her teapot so we could have something hot to drink. Then she carefully washed and wrapped the teapot and hid it under the kitchen sink so her husband wouldn't know she was drinking tea."

After over nine months in hospitals, Dad received an Honorable Discharge on October 25, 1945. He had served in the Army for four years and nine months. We all traveled back to Chicago for a joyful family reunion.

After the war, disabled veterans did not have an easy time of it. Cousins Carole Jane and Richard remember running to catch a street car in Chicago with their parents and my disabled dad. The conductor impatiently yelled for Dad to hurry. When he finally saw Dad with one arm, struggling to walk with his heavy leg brace, the conductor was ashamed and embarrassed. He apologized profusely for having hurried Dad.

The end of World War II brought great rejoicing in America. Cousin Richard remembers visiting at Verna's home in Chicago as a small boy, tearing up newspapers and throwing them out the window in celebration. He remembers taking a basket downstairs, picking up the shredded papers, going back upstairs, and tossing them out again and again. Following James' return, Agnes' husband Otto came home from Europe, and Frank Jr. came home from Guam.

Karolina was thankful her family survived another great challenge of life. The war made loved ones appreciate each other more, just as surviving the difficult days in West Virginia had made the Grabiecs appreciate each other. Light does shine brightest in the dark! With determination, love, and faith in God, they continued to have hope for a better future.

It is a wonderful thing about America—today all of us are free to make choices in our lives because there were, and still are, those willing to sacrifice, suffer, and even die to preserve our God-given freedoms. This was the dream of freedom Karolina had hoped for.

1945 Chicago Family Reunion[15]

Karolina with Her First Nine Grandchildren
Back: Earl, Audrey, Joey, Karolina, Jimmie Lou, Carole, Frannie
Front: Betty Jo, Nancy Lee, Richard

The smile on Karolina's face in this photo shows her joy and love for the blessing of each of her first nine grandchildren.

~

Back in Phoenix life drastically changed not only for Mom and Dad but also for two-year-old Nancy. She'd had her mother and her grandmother all to herself before Dad and I entered her life. Now she had to share them with two strangers. When Mom bathed her in the sink, Nancy turned her head and would not even look at her. When Mom had to leave Nancy so she could run errands, Nancy remembers waiting on Grandma's front doorsteps wondering if Mom was coming back.

After recovering from his war injuries, Dad got a job as Special Delivery Mail Carrier for the U. S. Postal Service in Phoenix. He kept that job until he retired. After thirty years, he was awarded a safe driving award, an especially significant honor considering he was a disabled veteran and drove with only one arm.

Mom and Dad bought a home at 1211 E. Cocopah near Karolina's home in Phoenix. At that time Cocopah Street was a dirt road, and an oil truck came by occasionally to oil it down to lessen the dust. Nancy and I remember running barefoot to the small corner grocery store with empty pop bottles to get money for gum or candy. In the summer when the ground was hot, we had to run to patches of shade or grass to cool our feet between our house, Grandma's house, and the store. In contrast, a strange memory Nancy has—even though it is rare for Phoenix—is that it snowed one year when we lived there. Nancy also remembers she hid her pennies in a wall of that house and did not remember to get them out when we moved—probably couldn't have anyway!

On August 14, 1946, at age twenty-seven, Dad was issued a prosthesis— an artificial arm and hand. Cousin Carole Jane came with us to Van Nuys, California, to help Mom take care of Nancy and me. Carole remembers how we would back up to Dad so he could pick us up with his one arm and rock us.

We then traveled to Colorado to see Dad's brother, John Hayden, his wife Bonnie, and our cousins Judy and Dixie. On other trips we went to Chickasha, Oklahoma, to see Dad's parents, Bertha and Herbert Hayden. We also traveled to see his sisters and their families—Madge and Gus Mitchell in Lincoln, Nebraska; Elsie and Bob Prince in Dallas, Texas; and Jessie and Archie Buchanan and our cousin Hayden Lee in Ft. Worth, Texas.

Sally Sue, Helen and James' third daughter, was born January 7, 1948. As more and more family members moved to Phoenix, Sally was the darling baby to hold and love at that time.

In 1950 we moved to our new Phoenix home in an area surrounded by citrus groves. There was no Lincoln Drive then; Glendale Avenue ended at 16th Street. We walked up a dirt road to our desert property at the foot of Squaw Peak, now known as Piestewa Peak. At that time it was considered "way out in northeast Phoenix" (now it is "central" Phoenix!). Dad discerned that for us this was the best place to be. Grandma Karolina loved to visit and sit out in the yard, looking at the beautiful irrigated yards or up at the palms, the mountain and the desert. They all were beautiful to her. (My brother, John, still owns that home today where we love to gather and talk about our memories.)

Arizona drew more family members over the next several years. Not only was it a beautiful place to live but they also wanted to be near their precious mother, Karolina. Mother's sister Annie and her family moved to Phoenix in 1951. In 1952 their sister Agnes and her family moved to Phoenix. I remember the huge truck as it arrived and meeting Uncle Otto. Even though he was a man of few words, he liked to tease us, and I remember his quiet stare scared me. I also remember there were lots of excited cousins running around Grandma Karolina's yard that day. Soon more family members moved to Arizona. Friends Mike Cernuska and his wife Mary also joined the Grabiecs in moving to Arizona.

Many changes were taking place in Phoenix at this time. I remember coming back from a trip with Mom and how different the city looked to me. It was growing fast. I was witnessing the beginning of the development explosion of Phoenix!

Arizona activities were especially enjoyable for our growing family. We often climbed up to Hole-in-the-Rock Mountain near Tempe, picnicked and played in the shade of palm-covered ramadas at South Mountain Park, and lingered to admire the spectacular sunsets and city lights of Phoenix at night. We visited the surrounding lakes and the Blue Bird Mine in Goldfield. Grandma liked to go for rides in the car but was nervous the time Dad drove us along the Apache Trail northeast of Phoenix.

Uncle Joe and Aunt Matreena remember going dancing with Mom and Dad at different "honky-tonks" in Arizona. They loved to dance, and Matreena remembers Dad calling it "cutting up the mustard!" Karolina enjoyed watching them dance western style at South Mountain Park. They played records or the radio and danced on the large concrete slabs—Mom with Dad, and then with us kids, doing a type of "line dance."

For keeping cool in the summers, Riverside Pool on South Central Avenue was a popular spot for the family. When it was not too hot, some went horseback riding at the Weldon Stables in South Phoenix in the 1950s. Mom loved to ride. She rode for the fun of it but also for her health. Her doctor told

Horse Posing with Mom in Arizona

her to ride after she almost died from jaundice after giving birth to her babies. What a wonderful therapy! One of our favorite photos of Mom is this one. She wrote to her sister, "Even the horse is posing for this photo!"

Willie often visited the Grabiecs in Arizona. I remember him as a tall, large-nosed, happy man. He made everyone laugh when he came around. He also enjoyed horseback riding at Papago Park with my mother and other family and friends.

Family members who did not move to Arizona still came to visit often. They wanted to share their lives and experiences–to laugh and cry together, sing and worship together, and just be there for each other as they always had been.

12

Karolina

Her children arise and call her blessed.
Proverbs 31:28a

Karolina was one of those people I call "my favorites." She was quiet, smart, and loved her husband, her children, and her grandchildren. She loved her Arizona neighbors Mrs. Wesson and Mrs. Bristow. She loved her friends and was a friend to all who knew her.

Karolina's faith was not diminished through her hardships but instead grew strong. The fruit of the Spirit of God could be observed in her manner and in her life—love, joy, peace, patience, kindness, goodness, faithfulness, gentleness, and self-control (Galatians 5:22-23). In 1952 at age sixty she was baptized into Christ by our minister, Reverend D. M. Peterson, at Stevenson Park Church of Christ in Phoenix. Karolina's faith was observed by her children, and it affected the way they saw the world. They could see that she felt the blessed sense of God's presence and His power which strengthened her. Her words "God is above us" declared it all.

A "homey" home was always made by Karolina with her love, hard work, and her children all around her. Every home she lived in was made loving and cozy by her influence. Everyone pitched in and had a part to play in keeping the family warm, fed, and together. "Many hands make light work," she taught them. A small yet energetic creek in West Virginia reminded me of Grandmother Karolina and how she kept her home bustling along. The creek and all the little streams make such a beautiful sound, gurgling, trickling down, and working their way along their individual paths. I feel the energy of my grandparents and their children in these streams.

Karolina knew instinctively how to raise her children. She learned from her parents and from experiencing a close relationship with her children—not from studying books. She knew how to be lovingly firm, yet gave them the space they needed to be creative. She respected their individual differences. Karolina taught them how to live fulfilled lives at various levels of prosperity. All her children loved and respected her when she was alive, and respect her memory today.

I remember many visits to Grandma's modest home. She always found something for the children to do. One summer Grandma gave us each a large branch from her chinaberry tree. We marched around the yard singing and doing whatever else kids do with large branches. On hot summer days she filled large wash tubs with cool water, and all the young cousins had so much fun playing in their undies, splashing, yelling, and running around the yard. This reminded Uncle Frank of how his mother bathed them in a tub in West Virginia when they were children. In her garden we ate her delicious fresh pomegranates, grapes, and figs. I also remember we played with her neighbor Mrs. Wesson's daughter, Nora, who had a barrel full of paper dolls.

On several occasions Grandmother Hayden visited us from Oklahoma. We listened to her play her harmonica while

Karolina with Helen's Girls

Kids in Grandma's Tubs 1948

Grandmothers Hayden and Grabiec

Grandma Karolina sang. She loved to sing "The Blue Skirt Waltz," in Polish, about a "girl dressed in blue . . . prettiest girl in the world . . . ,"Agnes sings, smiling. "She also sang a song about 'old engine number nine'." Often we would sing along with the two Grandmothers, learning songs and enjoying their love.

I was happy just being with Grandmother Karolina. She was so sweet and kind to us children. When I was with her I did not need a toy or a game. She did not need to take me anywhere. She was not able to go much, anyway suffering as she did with asthma.

I often

Grandma Karolina and Me with Her Dolls

My Favorite Doll

watched her sew and crochet many dolls and doll clothes. She made animals and hassocks shaped like elephants or horses for us to sit on. I still have my favorite doll she made for me as well as several others. She even taught me how to sew by hand and on her machine. She also taught me to crochet a simple belt, her hands and fingers quickly knotting the stitches.

Karolina and her children, my aunts and uncles, never sat around idle. Their lives exemplified the scriptures, "Whatever your hand finds to do, do it with all your might" (Ecclesiastes 9:10a) as well as "Whatever you do, work at it with all your heart, as working for the Lord, not for men" (Colossians 3:23). Working gave them pleasure—a sense of joy in accomplishment! The men worked hard at their jobs and then trimmed trees, built or fixed up their homes, and drove us wherever we needed to go. The women cleaned, gardened, cooked, or crocheted while they talked; they were always productive.

After the work was done, the women pierced each other's ears and cut and permed each other's hair. At age three my sister Nancy even took part when she drank the perm solution they were using, resulting in a trip to the hospital to have her stomach pumped!

Grandma Karolina raised chickens, and Little Nancy at about age two was intrigued with watching the chickens eating pebbles, so she tried eating pebbles, too! At age four she watched Dad catch and wring the necks of our dinner chickens one day. Nancy tried that also! She grabbed an unsuspecting chicken and swung it around by its neck. After being rescued from Nancy's little grip, the poor chicken wobbled around for a while but was OK—for the time being.

Every Sunday after church we met at Grandma's home for her delicious homemade chicken soup with dumplings or noodles. I remember watching Grandma as she plucked the chickens for dinner. I saw the feathers fly from her fingers—fast and nimble after years of practice. Her soup was the best—this is where chicken soup was perfected! Only once do I remember her straining the soup instead of the noodles. There must have been a lot of commotion that day with hungry kids and grand-kids running around in her two-room house!

I remember Grandma serving me some of her "zoop," as she called it with her Polish accent. And for some strange reason, when I was little, I thought that putting salt on it cooled it off. I also remember her reaction when I said, "This cup is dirty." It was not, though; it only had crumbs on the outside of it from her hardworking hands. I'll never forget how frustrated she looked at that moment. "I would not give you a dirty cup!" she scolded. This memory stays with me because I loved her so much, and I didn't mean to hurt her feelings.

Polish dishes were some of the favorite foods of Karolina's growing extended family. Aunt Matreena remembers Karolina taught her Polish songs and many delicious Polish recipes when she and Joe lived next door.

She learned to make *polisinki* (thin pancakes with jelly and cottage cheese), *pierogi* (yeast dough with cottage cheese, a plum, or other fillings in the center, boiled and fried with butter), *kapusta* (cabbage) with pork and gravy, and *kielbasa,* (Polish sausage) wrapped in bread dough and baked to a golden crust as the juices soaked into the bread surrounding it. Other recipes included *golabki* (stuffed cabbage rolls), and *kolaczki* (Polish pastry), which are my favorites!

I remember Grandma's quick hands turning and kneading the dough. Mom told us girls that kneading dough is good for the bustline. (My sister, Sally, said that kneading also helps counteract her carpel tunnel syndrome.)

Aunt Matreena remembers Karolina as a "humble, kind lady." She also was "as strong as a horse" as the old saying goes. "I worked hard when I was young," Karolina had told her. Even after she retired, Karolina still worked hard moving wood, sewing, plucking chickens, and cooking chicken noodle soup for the family visits every Sunday.

I still can envision Grandma sitting in her chair with her nylon stockings rolled at the top and twisted into a knot, her tired bunioned feet up, wearing her soft moccasins. I remember her holding a cup of coffee and struggling to breathe with her asthma. One day she told me to close my eyes. After a moment she said, "Jimmie Lou, you are going to have beautiful eyes!" She always made me feel so special. I'll never forget her.

Because of her severe asthma, Karolina had to give herself shots in her arms or in her legs. Her doctor also advised her to drink Coke syrup to stimulate her circulation. When she was too ill or too weak to give herself a shot, or her "needles" as she called them, Joe did it for her. One day she was having such a bad asthma attack, she turned blue. Dr. Stump stayed on the phone with Joe while he gave her one shot every five minutes until she came out of the attack. After four shots the color came back to her face. When Joe could no longer care for Karolina's personal needs, his sister Annie took care of her in her home.

~

Frank Grabiec Sr., Karolina's husband and my grandfather, was rarely discussed by Karolina and her children. His is another story, but in short, after he was released from the hospital in Weston, West Virginia, his sister, Frances Grabiec Kirkbride and her daughter, Ann, came from La Junta, Colorado, to pick him up. He found work in the coal mines near Oak Creek. He once again had family members not too far away and started a new life. On May 16, 1944, Frank Grabiec became a citizen of the United States of America and was awarded a Certificate of Naturalization.

Frank continued working as a loader on the graveyard shift. He is pictured in the photo below, in the front row, far right with twelve of the thirty-seven total on his shift. His health eventually failed due to black lung and

Frank Sr. on Graveyard Shift

related conditions, so he applied for retirement at the end of 1954. He had given many years of his life to the coal mines—seven to the Simpson Creek Collieries Company of Galloway, West Virginia, from August 1918 to March 1925 and more than sixteen years to the Moffat, Arrowhead, and Dunn Coal Companies in Oak Creek, Colorado, from September 1938 to December 1954.

However, after twenty-three years of hard labor in the coal mines of America, Frank never got a pension. According to the

Frank Sr. with Karolina

mining officials his work had to be consecutive, and with twelve years recuperating from head injuries and his nervous breakdown, he was denied any benefits.

In 1953, after many years of separation, his sister, Frances, and his daughter Frances helped him and Karolina to be reunited for a short time. Frank briefly got reacquainted with his grown children during several short trips to Chicago, Illinois; La Junta, Colorado; Phoenix, Arizona; and Oak Creek, Colorado. He and Karolina realized, however, that it still would not work out between them and decided it would be better to continue living apart. Karolina spent her final days living in Annie's home. Before she died, her husband Frank Sr. came to see her one more time.

"Karolina, you was a good woman," he told her in his broken English. After his visit the family took him to the train station, and they watched the train pull out with him for what was to be the last time. Frank Jr. remembers seeing the long train go by as he drove home down Grand Avenue. Only he knows the thoughts that were running through his mind as he watched his father leave again.

One day Grandma Karolina told my mother that she had seen a vision of a cross on the wall. She knew something had happened to her mother, Mary, back in Karvina, Czechoslovakia. Later she found out that the vision had come when her mother had died. Karolina had never seen her mother again after leaving Karvina in 1913. Karolina died on February 11, 1955. Now they are together for eternity!

At the end of August, 1956, in Oak Creek, Colorado, Frank Sr. and his friend Olivia Wilson were returning in his pickup truck from a shopping trip in Steamboat Springs. Suddenly a speeding teenage driver ran them off what was then a narrow gravel road on a very sharp curve, causing them to roll several times down a steep embankment and landing upside down. Far away in Phoenix a bright red flash woke my mother from a deep sleep that same night. She knew something had happened to her father in Colorado—they had always been very close.

Frank Sr. with Helen

With no ambulance available in Oak Creek at the time, Frank was taken to the small hospital by a vehicle from Hageman's Garage. He had suffered a broken back and other injuries. Olivia was not badly injured. Joseph and Verna came from Phoenix to be with their father for the last few days of his life. When they arrived they found that he had not yet been cleaned up from the crash, had dust in his hair, and had not been shaved. Verna got a razor and shaved him and helped the nurse clean him up.

Frank Sr. told Joseph to take the fish that was in his freezer. He also pleaded with Joseph, saying, *"Piwo! Piwo!"* (pronounced "pē' vo"). Joe believes he was asking for a shot of whiskey. At the time, however, Verna thought it best not to give it to him. Joseph regrets that he did not get it for him, realizing that his father must have been in severe pain. Frank Grabiec Sr. died September 2, 1956, and is buried in Oak Creek, Colorado.

I vaguely remember being with Grampa Frank and my mother for one visit in Phoenix and one in Oak Creek. He and I couldn't speak to each other—I didn't know Polish and he didn't know much English. Even though he had less than two years of retirement before he died, my mother was thankful that his last years seemed to be happy with Olivia and his Slavic friends in Oak Creek. I only wish I could have known him better. I remember him to be a quiet man, and even though he was often absent as a father, I will always love him, as did Karolina and Helen.

It's hard to say goodbye. I was almost ten when Grandmother Karolina died in 1955. I'll never forget running to the end of her driveway, sitting on the ground in the dark and looking back toward her house. I was so sad. I stared at her house from the end of the long driveway and thought, "I'll never forget this moment.

1955 Grandma Karolina's Driveway

I'll never forget this vision of Grandma's house without her. I'll never forget how sad I feel." I never have. I still cry today when I think of that vision.

Some have looked in wonder at Karolina and her family–amazed at their accomplishments after all the hardships they went through. But hardships only made the Grabiecs stronger, more innovative, more independent, and more unified with family love and loyalty. Their faith was also strengthened as they trusted God to sustain them through it all.

Part Four: Legacy of Love

13

Helen's Spirit

A cheerful heart is good medicine.
Proverbs 17:22a

The spirit of love, determination, and faith that lived in Grandmother Karolina also lived in my mother, Helen. She was intelligent, pensive, thoughtful, intuitive, and caring. Her spirit was strong and made even stronger through her hardships. I think her ornery streak made her interesting. Aside from her respect for God, for her parents, and for her husband, she didn't do what others said she should do unless she really wanted to. She had a mind of her own. She had to, to be a survivor—one of the *real survivors*!

Mother was a wonderful person to know. I treasure all the memories of her love and wit. She gave much and demanded little. She was an inspiration to all who knew her.

Helen Walking in Phoenix

Love and laughter inspired and delighted my mother. She had the special gifts of humor and optimism. She saw her cup as half full, not half empty;

she saw the patch of blue on a gray day. If she could do something about the unattractive aspects of life, she did. But she knew when it was out of her hands, and then she would pray for God's intervention.

Mother saw the good in people and was not judgmental. She also saw the possibility for good in most situations. When I saw the movie "Pollyanna," I thought of Mom and how she viewed and reacted to life. When she was young, many saw her as the "life of the party." With her optimistic spirit, she was happy—she laughed, sang, and danced.

Mom's spirit shone in her eyes, in her musical, lyrical laugh, and in her sense of humor, her little quips and spontaneous wittiness! She demonstrated loving patience—smiling, her eyes twinkling.

Relationships came naturally for my mother, Helen. She could identify with people from all walks of life. She had had many experiences from which she learned and remembered. As one uncle described her to me, "Your mother was a saint. Even though she was stubborn at times, she helped everyone."

Simple country folk and the simple way of life were easy for her to love. She financially supported the Christian Appalachian Project because she knew from experience that the needs of the people are great. She also knew how a little money went such a long way in their simple way of life. It was used for necessities, not luxuries.

Mom had empathy for the less fortunate. She and her siblings were grateful for those who had helped them in the hard times. They always found ways to reciprocate by helping others. Mother helped those in need whether or not they would ever be able to give anything back. It is easy to love those who love us back, but Mom showed us how to "love the unlovely," which is the *real* love that Jesus teaches. What good is it if we only love those who love *us* (Matthew 5:46)?

Remembering her days of poverty, Mom commented, "We live like royalty! We have hot and cold running water, bathrooms, heaters and coolers, and oranges all year long. Even the price of food is not what it costs to grow it—we have to be thankful!"

The materially rich who were poor in spirit also craved Mother's time and love. She could understand their loneliness and their need to be appreciated. She fulfilled a need that money and security had not met. And she had a lot to give—she had a big heart, and it was a heart of gold.

Her intuitive spirit helped her to see problems from a unique point of view. Because she loved to read, Mom had an article to quote about most topics of conversation. She seemed to be the family counselor at times. People called her often to share their problems and get her perspective. She was a good listener. She was very careful, though, to stay out of the middle between husband and wife, saying, "I'm your friend, but don't put me in the middle." Even with close loved ones, she had a way of being objective—of removing herself from the situation. That was really amazing to me—how she could *do* that.

She taught us not to cling desperately to relationships but to trust God with them. One great piece of advice she gave was that love is like holding sand. If you try to hold it with a tight grip, it goes right through your fingers. But if you hold sand gently, you can hold a lot more of it and for a much longer time.

Faith was the foundation for my mother's spiritual strength. Her faith in God grew as she matured as a Christian. She reconfirmed her faith at age thirty-three when she was baptized into Christ on May 5, 1953, by our minister, Reverend D. M. Peterson, at Stevenson Park Church of Christ in Phoenix.

We loved that little church in South Phoenix. Mom and her sisters helped teach Sunday school classes, brought us to the potluck dinners, and sang solos, duets, and group selections. I sang my first solo, "He Shall Feed His Flock," in this church when I was nine. My sister Nancy and

Little Hayden Sisters

I were baptized there in 1958 by the new minister at that time, Reverend Jim Piercy. One of my favorite memories about that church is that we always ended the worship service with the song, "God Be With You 'til We Meet Again." We still often bless each other with "God be with you," when we part.

When our family moved to another home in Phoenix we became founding members of First Christian Church, which was closer to home. Reverend Dr. William S. Boice was our senior pastor for many years. Children were a major focus for this church, and my sisters and brothers and I went to many camp sessions and retreats at the United Christian Youth Camp in Prescott. When an uncle commented that our church would fall apart if our gifted and devoted minister ever left, Mother reminded him we are to put our faith in God, not in man.

Mom's trust in God gave her peace at times when there was no peace. Her joy came from the Lord, not from her earthly circumstances or possessions. Her faith was unwavering, as was her mother Karolina's. She took pride in doing what she believed was right and doing it for God. While growing up we could see that her confidence came from this firm foundation.

That's why we called her when we needed a "faith lift" once in a while. We usually did not get sympathy, if that is what we were looking for. Mom somehow saw the other side of the situation and told us why it wasn't so bad after all. "God is good!" she said often.

Mother's life of music was one of intense emotional involvement. With her beautiful voice, she spent countless hours rehearsing and performing with the Phoenix Opera Company. She was a founding member of this highly trained and professional group, first known as the Phoenix Symphonic Choir.[16] She performed in operas such as Guiseppe Verdi's *La Traviata* and light operas[17] such as Cole Porter's *Can Can*. Occasionally performances were given at the Encanto Park Band Shell where we watched, sitting on the outdoor lawn on cool evenings in Phoenix.

Mom also sang solos and in large and small groups at church, especially during the holidays—so we sang also! At home Mom would often burst forth with a song relating to almost any topic of conversation. She seemed to have a song for everything!

Phoenix Symphonic Choir (Helen 2nd from right)

For some of her rehearsals, I remember Dad driving us all the way out to Apache Junction where we waited while Mom rehearsed. Her music director, Lois Albright, taught her to practice a technique until it felt natural, and then, when performing, to forget it. She showed us how "practice makes perfect."

My introduction to the evil of the prejudice of the 1950s occurred when Mom shared with me her experiences with her black friend in the opera company. When they wanted to go out to eat after rehearsals her friend said, "You know we'll have to walk and we will have to eat at the Y." She was not allowed to use the restroom in many places and not allowed to ride the bus. On one occasion their music director, Lois, had to sneak a black opera star visiting from New York into a Phoenix "whites-only" hotel. It took determination to defy evil in those days.

Mother had a high regard for her director. Lois and her husband, M. W. Billingsley,[18] composed the three-scene, Opera in One Act, *Hopitu* which

AN EPOCH

of

"The Hopi, a people whose civilization flourished on the American Continent when England was uninhabited."

Dr. J. Walter Fewkes, Bureau of American Ethnology,
Smithsonian Institution, Washington, U.S.A.

•

LOIS ALBRIGHT has captured their ancient chants

in her Opera in One Act, Three scenes—

H·O·P·I·T·U

(Hopi People)

•

Founded upon Primitive Legends

Libretto by M. W. Billingsley, White Mungwee

(Thirty Years with the Hopi)

•

HOPI CHANTS and DANCES
for the
First Time in Musical History

Hopitu Program

presented the Hopi chants and dances. Since Mother had one of the lead roles in this opera, and knowing how ill her mother, Karolina, was, she talked Lois into having an understudy for her part. This was the first and only time Lois agreed to have an understudy for one of her performers.

"Don't you know you have children?" I chided as Mom packed and got ready to leave for her cross-country singing tour. At age nine I didn't know I should have been proud of her instead!

On the way to New York, Mother got the call she dreaded from Phoenix. Her dear mother, Karolina, had died. Mother's grief was unimaginable. She immediately came home to be with her family. The production went on without her and was performed at Carnegie Hall in New York on the evening of February 16, 1955.

Over the years her sadness was eased with the help of God, her family, and her church. Hymns and other Christian music were very healing to her. She and her sisters had beautiful voices which blended well, and they sang often for worship services and at family gatherings. They had many favorite hymns.[19]

Almost two years after her mother died, Helen and Jim's first son, **Herbert Thomas,** was born November 4, 1956, and almost two years after that, their second son, **John Robert,** was born July 5, 1958. They brought happiness back into Mother's heart and blessed the whole family.

Mom was happiest with her music and when she was with her family and friends. I remember how

Helen and Opera Friends
(From left) Thea, Alice, Elizabeth, Helen, (in photo, Lucille)

much she enjoyed small group rehearsals in our home. In preparing for rehearsals and lessons Mother practiced her vocal scales and songs at home. The neighbors would occasionally mention, "I heard your mother singing the other day as I walked by."

As children we liked to imitate her vocalizing. Mom encouraged us to take voice, piano, and other music lessons. Besides having our piano, she bought us several other instruments including a guitar, a violin, a baritone horn, and drums. We sang in church, and she took us to classical concerts. We all grew up loving music. Some of us sang in musical groups in grade school, high school, and college.

My father, James, was the love of Mother's life. They had truly been through much together. Dad supported Mom in most things she wanted to do, but at other times, respect for his wishes caused her pain. When he had denied her permission to see a performance by Jeanette MacDonald, one of her favorite singers, she was very upset. When he saw how disappointed she was, he asked, "If it meant that much to you, why didn't you insist on going?" She replied, "I was not raised that way." She had been taught to be respectful and not to be selfishly demanding. Now she had to learn to be resolute if she earnestly wanted something.

Mom and Dad had taught us to respect our parents also, however, so a similar situation occurred when my sister Nancy wanted to go to an art college out of state. Dad said, "No," and she didn't beg or demand to go. He was surprised when she was upset about his decision. Again he told Mother, "If she really wanted to go, she would have insisted." So now we children also had to learn how to be more determined in expressing ourselves.

Learning to drive was something Mother had long been determined to try. So, over his objections, she "insisted." He was so irritated about this decision that he took her to the Motor Vehicle Department and left her there! She decided it was not worth the trouble it would cause and took the bus home. She never did learn to drive—nor did five of her six sisters.

So, if Dad was not available to take us, we rode the bus, walked, or got a ride from family members, neighbors, or friends to the pool, church, school events, shops, or the homes of family and friends. But the funny thing was, when my brother Herb was learning to drive, Dad had Mom ride with him as the adult rider, even though she didn't drive! I'm sure she loved going around town with her son driving her! Later in life we drove her wherever she wanted to go, and I'm thankful for every moment I spent with her.

After work, Dad often ate dinner after we ate dinner. He could relax more that way. Weekends with five kids, of course, were hectic. Dad retired early, at age forty-two, due to a heart murmur, besides all the damage to his health from war injuries. He and Mom decided to regard Mondays as their "day off." When we all went off to school, their day off started—at least for a few hours!

Hospitality was a natural for Mother, having been raised in the large Grabiec family. Her hospitality was shown almost daily not only to individuals and small groups but often at family picnics, family parties, and birthday celebrations in our home. We also gathered at the ramada my Dad built on our desert property overlooking Phoenix. We always had tubs of various flavors of pop and watermelon, as well as lots of fried chicken or hamburgers and hot dogs. We enjoyed hiking the mountain and watching the amazing sunsets. We always had marshmallows for the campfire at night as we watched the city lights and the stars. We especially enjoyed the fireworks on the Fourth of July.

Mother took pleasure in many facets of life and praised God in thankfulness for all her blessings. She not only appreciated music and family, but she loved to learn. She was an avid reader and very inquisitive. She collected many books, magazines and newspapers, and especially enjoyed learning new words. (Mom laughed when her good friend, Jean, misused *her* big words!) She enjoyed watching educational programs as well as classic movies and comedies.

As we all grew up and left home, Mom's determined spirit and love of learning inspired her to continue her education. At age fifty-two she started to take college classes at Maricopa Technical College in downtown Phoenix. She enjoyed her classes and loved "hanging out" in the Student Center, drinking coffee and talking to the other students, young and old. She often gave students money for a Coke or a snack.

Mom graduated with two Associate of Arts Degrees—one in Construction

Drafting and the other in General Studies. Her grandson, Nick, graduated from kindergarten the same night Mom was graduating. She was so excited about Nick's little graduation program that she forgot to go to her own!

Technology and mechanics fascinated my mother. She was ahead of her time with her interest in studying solar energy, different types of solar panels, and solar home building ideas. She owned some vacant land at the base of Piestewa Peak and wanted to build some solar homes there but never did. However, she was happy that a nearby street was named "Solar Drive." Now her son, my brother Herb, is working on the cutting edge of renewable energy technologies.

Other technological devices Mom was fond of were her Sony Watchman mini TV and the remote headphones for her main TV. Being mechanically inclined, Mom bought repair manuals of all types and enjoyed the challenge of repairing her old irons, radios, sewing machines, and whatever else needed fixing.

Love of the great outdoors drew Mother as it did when she was a child. We visited the Petrified Forest, Painted Desert, and other places of interest in Arizona. We went on many family camping and fishing trips at Horseshoe and Bartlett Lakes near Phoenix. Mom loved camping, and in the summer we occasionally slept outside at home in the back yard. I remember looking at the stars and the Milky Way at night before the city lights faded them out. There was no freeway noise, and it was so quiet!

In the back yard Mom loved the red rose bush Dad planted for her. She also loved the roses growing in my yard three blocks away. On my way to work I often took her the prettiest rose I could find. One year Mom and I took Aunt Frances a large beautiful multicolored bouquet of my roses. Mother was amazed that they lasted over a week! I have planted new rose bushes in her memory, but roses will never again be as beautiful to me as they were when she was living.

Mother's love of birds was instilled in all of us. During the last few years of Mom's life, a hummingbird made her nest on a clip-type clothes hanger on the awning outside her back door. We quietly watched all the activities from the kitchen window. The bird returned to that nest for several years. What a blessing it was that this took place when it did, since Mother was housebound.

One of Mother's favorite birds was the red cardinal. When she saw one in Phoenix, it reminded her of her mother, Karolina. My sister Nancy recently saw one in Dewey, Arizona, and it followed her as she went from putting her dog in his run to watering the garden. We both believe God sent it as a cheerful reminder that Mom's spirit lives on in us today and that she will always be with us.

Style gives way to creativity. In Chicago Mom learned to love style—stylish clothes, hats, gloves, and shoes. In Arizona, Mom looked great wearing her size six jodhpur riding pants. She also looked stylish in her boots, slacks, dresses, or western Indian-style dresses with her beautiful silver concho belt. One of her favorite fragrances was Elizabeth Arden's "Bluegrass." We knew she liked it, so she often got too many perfumes and powders of this one fragrance.

Even on a limited budget, Mother liked our home to look beautiful also. But with a creative family of seven she finally "gave up" to let us do our thing. Pretty draperies, lamps, couches, and a player piano (complete with music rolls) were still there, but the "clutter" of books, music, instruments, art projects, sewing projects, and cooking projects was endless. (I think that is why Dad loved working for hours outside in the yard—even in the Arizona summers!) Mother, too, had interesting hobbies and projects to do all over the house and yard. Now I see this in myself and my siblings today!

Little treasures were all Mother wanted as far as material things go. One favorite collection of hers was objects made of colored glass, and she especially liked red, blue, and amber. She also had an orange glass punch bowl with blue, yellow, and green cups, which I treasure today. I use it now at family gatherings and think of her.

Humor was essential while living in the Hayden household. With Mom's wisdom came her unique and quick sense of humor. She enjoyed reading books like *The Neurotic's Notebook* by Mignon McLaughlin and the humorous sections of *The Reader's Digest*. She laughed often, and some misunderstood it, thinking they were being mocked or laughed *at*. But I think she was often laughing at herself. When she became forgetful as she got older, she chuckled, "My mind—how I miss it!" She occasionally had a smug smile but more often a bright open smile. I think she knew that even God has a sense of humor!

Even when Mom was occasionally criticized by Dad, she often saw humor in his comments. She enjoyed analyzing his perspective and was able to look at both sides of the situation. Frustrated, Dad chided, "You analyze long and analyze wrong." But I found her to be right most of the time!

After Mom returned from being away for several months visiting her sisters, Dad greeted her with, "While you were gone, I realized I still love you." She laughed and replied, "*I* knew that!"

Mother was one of the happiest people I ever knew. She was happy because she put others first, she surrounded herself with family and friends, she did not feel a sense of competition with others, and she forgave quickly and easily. I remember her reaction when I apologized to her one day. She simply said, "Oh, that's OK!"

Mother's cheerful spirit showed even in her walk—her bouncy quick step—(especially when wearing her Capezio dancing shoes!) She knew that a cheerful heart is good medicine (Proverbs 17:22a). She spread good humor and love to others, and she did not let critical or jealous persons quench her spirit.

Mom not only loved to sing, but she also loved to dance. I enjoyed watching her and Dad dancing western style at Bud Brown's Barn in Phoenix. After Dad died in 1977, Mom continued dancing with the Merry Makers and other senior groups.

Family unity was cherished by Mother as it had been by her mother. Mom believed, as her brother Frank did, that "What is good for one should be good for all." She taught us to be kind to each other, because some day we would be separated and miss each other, which indeed has happened. All her life she cheerfully took care of loved ones in need, often having to walk or take the bus to their homes.

In many ways Mother taught us to put family first. For years a friend had invited Mother, but not her children, to go up to the friend's cabin in the pines; Mother refused to go without us. At another time she said, "Treat family like company, and treat company like family." She also said, "When hiring a family member to do a job, pay them as much or more than you would pay a stranger, not less." Mother also encouraged us to "Look nice for your family members as well as for others."

Even though Mother and I were often at odds when I was a teenager, later in life we were best of friends. Since she loved to travel, she agreed to go with me to pick up my stranded car in Douglas, Arizona. We took the Greyhound Bus and had so much fun laughing and talking. We were talking about the ups and downs of life and for some reason I said to her, "We just have to get our faith lifted!" We laughed and laughed. She was such great company; always ready to laugh when analyzing life! We also enjoyed another trip together, this time to New Mexico to pick up my brother's stranded car. We flew to Albuquerque and started out the next day for Phoenix. That was an enjoyable trip, too, laughing and talking all the way. We had only one vapor-lock in the mountains and got home OK.

Since I left home I have always lived in or near Phoenix. I probably didn't visit my mother as often as I could have or should have. I remember when I stopped by one day to visit, she opened the door and said, "Oh! I *do* have daughters, *don't* I!" She was happy to see me, and I made an effort to "stop by" more often after that. At that time my retired Dad and two brothers lived at home. "Even the dog is a boy," she said.

Now it's my turn to wish *my* daughter would "stop by" and see me more often! But she is currently teaching in South Korea for the U. S. Department of Defense, so that's not likely to happen!

When honoring God, Mom knew He would honor her (1 Samuel 2:30b), and He did. She taught us right from wrong–no grey areas. Whether or not we chose to do the right thing as young adults was our decision. She knew she could not make decisions for us. She learned from her mother to "live and let live." She knew we would have to make decisions for our own lives and would also be responsible for the consequences. She taught us that Jesus gives us *hope* for today as well as for the future, and without hope in Him we are of all men, most miserable (1 Corinthians 15:19 KJ).

With a calm manner like her mother's, Mom never seemed to have to rush. She seemed to be quietly preparing every day for opportunities in the future. When an opportunity arose, she was ready in spirit for whatever needed to be done. One of her favorite quotes was, "Faith is the soul that reaches forth to God and never returns empty."

In the 1980s, after moving back into my mother's neighborhood, I walked to a nearby newly-built church to visit for the first time. I was surprised to find my widowed mother sitting by herself in the sanctuary. She had walked over to visit for the first time also! Coincidence?

Mom's large black family Bible is well worn and falling apart. When she became a Christian, she studied the Word avidly, but she never underlined or wrote in it. After thinking about this for a while, I realized that she was raised in a generation in which books were cherished and not written in. When someone once commented on her Bible falling apart, she said, "The Bible that is falling apart belongs to someone who isn't."

Throughout her life, Mom had learned to put her trust only in God. She taught us that if we read this book, the Bible, we would be free! As a teen I wasn't sure about that, but now I know what she meant. It makes me free in spirit which means totally without bondage of any kind! Two more of Mother's favorite books were *Mere Christianity* by C. S. Lewis and *The Christian's Secret of a Happy Life* by Hannah Whitall Smith, written in 1875.

Whether inherited or learned, the strength of her spirit lives on in us. My passion and persistence in writing this book is a reflection of her spirit living on in me!

14

The Power of the Home

He blesses the home of the righteous.
Proverbs 3:33b

The power of the home cannot be underestimated. Education and experience helped my sisters and brothers and me to know what we wanted to do and how to do it, but our family made us who we are. The spirit of faith, determination, and love shown by Grandmother Karolina and our mother, Helen, had an immeasurable affect on us.

All our lives Mom firmly and quietly taught us right from wrong and that God is the ultimate authority. He would hold us accountable for our decisions. Like Karolina she knew that a gentle answer turns away wrath as taught in Proverbs 15:1. She was never judgmental and knew when to let us make our own mistakes—when to let go. She modeled how to make constructive decisions by making them for her own life.

Values of honesty and truth were taught in our household, and Mother encouraged us to keep our minds pure. She believed in the value of Philippians 4:8, "Whatever is true, whatever is noble, whatever is right, whatever is pure, whatever is lovely, whatever is admirable—if anything is excellent or praiseworthy—think about such things."

Mom and Dad had our best interests at heart. While Dad worked, Mom was a full-time homemaker and was always there for us. We did not have to rely on our peers, TV, movies, music, and radio—people who don't necessarily care about us—more than our parents who loved us the most and wanted what was best for our lives. I did not always appreciate their correction and direction, but I am thankful for it today.

We were discouraged from being loud or dramatic to get attention, as if we were "on stage." "Sit still; be silent, and *they* will find *you*," is an old Polish saying Nancy remembers Mom telling her. Yelling was not allowed in our home. If we wanted to speak to someone in another room, we couldn't just holler out for them. We had to go to them and say what we wanted to say. When we girls were young, Mom had firm expectations. We were expected to simply obey. When our parents asked us to do something, we were expected to respond immediately. It was unthinkable to say "No" or "Later" to a request. Mom taught us that "Work is love in action."

Parenting with patience and love was in Mother's spirit as it had been in her mother, Karolina's. These contributed to her success in the home. Even though she took time for herself and her singing career, she never made her family feel neglected. She was there for us and gave us the freedom to be ourselves.

Mom had many opportunities to practice patience with me. When I was two, I was sick one night and had thrown up all over my bed and pajamas. After she had cleaned everything up and put clean pajamas on me, I insisted on buttoning each button by myself. She was so tired, but she patiently waited for me to do it. (She reminded me of it several times later in life, however, when she wanted me to know how determined I am!)

When I was five, the neighbor called Mom and asked her if she knew I was walking around on the roof. After getting me down she asked, "Don't you remember me telling you never to get up on the roof?" I said, "I remember it now, but I didn't remember it then." What's a mother to do?

Another opportunity for Mom to be patient with me was right before leaving for church on a Sunday morning. I went out into our garden and ate some chives. Mother was so irritated, but what could she do? She just asked me why in the world would I do such a thing, and I really didn't know except that I love chives!

When my brother John was a toddler, he demonstrated his determined spirit. We had asked Mom what she wanted for Christmas, and she said, "All I want for Christmas is for Johnny to be potty-trained." He heard her remark, and from that day on, he was.

When John was about seven, he was mad at Mom for some reason and called her "an elephant." She thought for a second and replied with a smile, "Then you're my *baby* elephant!" A good sense of humor always helps!

Family pets were also loved and patiently cared for as we were growing up. I remember that the Grabiec family's long-time friend, Ann Lichner, told Mom she was amazed that her children fed the cat even before they ate their own breakfast.

We occasionally took in lost puppies—a Dalmatian, a poodle, and a mix. When "Blue," our Australian Shepard, got loose, Mom would have to take a bit of food and walk down the street, and he would always come to her. I don't think she even wanted a dog, but of course, like most moms, she took good care of him.

When I was on a college vacation break Mom let me keep a co-worker's parakeet, "Tweety Baby," for two weeks. Even though his cage was covered with a blanket, he whistled the "wolf whistle" in the middle of the night and made me jump. She laughed.

School situations were handled with tactful determination. When we were young we usually loved to go to school. And when we didn't, Mom knew how to motivate us. She did not pressure us to go to school but made us see that it was an alternative. When I wanted to stay home from school one day, she thought a moment and then said cheerfully, "Good! Today we can move furniture and wash the walls!" Of course I went to school instead, and I never asked to stay home from school again! She made me see that there *are* alternatives. I saw that I was accountable for my choices as well as for their consequences.

When John was away from home and in college having one of those difficult and discouraging days, he called Mom. She said, "Don't worry. You can come home." When he realized this *was* entirely possible, he decided to stay in school. It was not what he wanted for his life.

Mother would let us stay home from school if we were sick or tired, or if our grandparents or company came from out of town to visit. We also took time off to travel and visit grandparents or other family members. She occasionally let us have a "day off" if we had a bad morning, but we could not use that as an excuse from school and later go out with our friends. We had to stay in bed or just sit quietly in our room. There never was a phone or TV in our rooms, so we usually slept or read books. She took us to the library often, and we always had many good books around.

Mom and Dad's consistent awareness of language helped us do well in English classes. They did not use, nor did they allow us to use, slang. We had to speak correctly. When I was a little girl and could not get down from the top of the swing set in the back yard, I yelled, "Hey, Daddy, come help me down!" He came over to help, but first he had to lecture me on the impoliteness of saying "Hey!" At another time I came home from a high school football game and described it as a "lousy" game. Dad made me get the dictionary and look up the word "louse." I was surprised it was an insect—singular for "lice!"

For reading class I remember getting bogged down trying to read *Jane Eyre* for a book report assignment. Mom took the book and started reading it to me. That did it. I got interested again and finished the book myself.

1962 The Hayden Family

Disciplining teens was another challenge for Mom which she handled with loving determination. "If you sass me one more time, you're grounded," Mom said calmly but firmly. I knew the family was going on a picnic, and I knew they would not possibly leave me behind. I did sass "one more time," and I'll never forget them driving off without me! I stayed with Uncle Joe that day and learned that Mother said what she meant and meant what she said.

On another occasion I was sick, so Mom would not let me go to the school carnival with her and the rest of the family. I was so mad I screamed, "I *hate* you!" She just turned, looked at me, and calmly said, "That's a decision *you'll* have to make," and walked out the door. It took all the punch out of my fit of anger and left me with much food for thought.

When she was helping me with my hair one night as I was getting ready for a prom, I was irritated, impatient, and insulting to her. She looked at me and quietly asked, "How can such a pretty girl be so mean?" Just as Karolina had disciplined her children years earlier, Mom's calm manner and few words were effective. I can still hear the sound of her voice and never forgot her question. She reminded me that "Beauty is as beauty does."

A few of the other unforgettable phrases Mom used were:

"Watch your tongue."

"Watch your tone of voice."

"That behavior is going to come to a screeching halt!"

She once grounded me, saying, "That will fix your clock!"

In correcting us for teasing, Mom told us, "A little bit goes a long way." In disciplining with humor, she said, "Don't look at me with that tone of voice."

"You're not going to a fashion show!" she said when we spent too much time primping in front of the mirror in the bathroom. She taught us it was fine to look good but to also be modest and humble, which honors God and our parents.

If I was upset by a critical remark, she simply said, "If the shoe fits...."

I never remember Mom spanking us, but I do remember her telling me to go out into the back yard "to find a switch." I looked and looked for hours, and amazingly enough I could not find one. But I sure had a lot of time to think about why I was out there!

Creativity was fostered in our home. Mom let us have our projects throughout the house. One Christmas, Herb sewed together so many socks that his Christmas stocking went all the way down the hall and into his bedroom. I don't think she filled it full, but the stocking was unforgettable!

We had fun with our cousins as we dressed up in wigs, hats, old dresses, shoes, purses, and old colorful strings of beads and other costume jewelry. She didn't seem to mind the mess. We often played records, danced, and had a blast! But afterwards, Mom did not like to reciprocate by letting us go spend the night at others' homes when they had spent the night at ours. For some reason she always preferred us to be home.

Dating was not allowed until we were sixteen. I'm sure Mom prayed a lot in those days. An uncle told Mom, "You have a big responsibility with your three teenage girls." She responded, "You have just as much of a responsibility with your boys!" Mother taught us never to date someone we would not consider marrying. Another piece of advice she gave us was, "If you think there's a chance you might regret it, don't do it." One funny thing I remember is when it was time to say goodnight to our boyfriends, Mom flipped the porch light off and on!

Mom was determined that her family members should live full and healthy lives. She knew Proverbs 14:1, "The wise woman builds her house, but with her own hands the foolish one tears hers down." She built up her home by learning and then sharing her wisdom with us. Her wise tactics and tips were based on wisdom from her parents, from her life experiences, and from her study of the Scriptures. She was a good listener, was analytical, and loved a challenge. She experienced many challenges in her lifetime, and because she turned to God, the source of all wisdom, these challenges made her stronger and wiser, just as they had done for her mother, Karolina.

Homemaking skills were taught to us by Mother in a firm, creative, and loving way. Even though she often did her vacuuming and other chores late at night after long rehearsals with the opera company, during the day she still took the time to teach us how to work also. Giving us small tasks as children, she taught us skills useful for a lifetime.

Mom also used her sense of humor as Karolina must have done. When we were teenagers, she told us she and her sisters used to argue over who got to clean the house because it made their cheeks rosy for their boyfriends. "Really?" we wondered. We all learned to be good workers and have never had trouble getting or keeping good jobs.

Besides teaching us, "Read the Bible and you'll be free," Mom also said, "Do your chores and you'll be free." She later added to this by saying, "Don't even ask if you can go out until your work is finished. Then you can ask, and I can still say no." So Nancy organized us sisters by making a master list of all the jobs. We took turns choosing jobs and made our own lists on tiny 1" x 2" scraps of paper. (Maybe the small paper made it look like less work to us.) When washing the dishes, however, Nancy told Mom I broke a dish every time I did the dishes. Mom responded, "Well, she is still going to do the dishes."

Mom taught us that if Dad needed something to be done while he was at work, we should do that first. Then if everything didn't get done, at least his few requests would be done before he got home. When he told Mom he did not want to cause a "ruckus" by asking us to do something, she suggested that he write it down on a note, and she would give it to whoever needed to do the job. I think he liked that idea, because occasionally we got a note, written in Dad's handwriting. We could not complain or argue about it, nor would we dare ignore it! It seemed more important, I think, just being in writing and in *his* writing.

After doing what Dad requested, Mom taught us to do the next three most important things. She also suggested we do the hardest chores first.

In trying to have a strategy for a neater home with a family of seven, Mom occasionally announced, "There's going to be a new rule around here." One new rule was "P.I.B." "When you're finished with something and have it in your hand, put it back where it belongs. Then you don't have to handle it twice by picking it up again later." I still think of "P.I.B."

Mother could make light of a tough situation with humor at times. When a neighbor suggested that Mom needed a dishwasher, Mom replied, "I have three—and they sing!" Once as Mom looked around the house at all the projects, she remarked, "God has given me five children and they are all artists. Couldn't one of them have been a housekeeper?"

Mother knew Matthew 25:21b taught that if we take care of what we have,

God will bless us with more. For as long as she was able to, Mom took good care of our home. I remember her saying "Everything off!" when we cleaned the kitchen counters. Later with her creative and busy family, our home got more and more cluttered. But somehow Mom always knew where everything was. I remember when her sister Annie came over and found something she needed, she told Mom, "Your house is a gold mine!"

The following are just a few more of Mom's helpful homemaking tips:

"Leave a room neater than you found it."

"Have a place for everything and everything in its place."

"If you lose something, start cleaning and you will find it."

"Use the right tool for the job. It makes the job easier."

"Don't force it if something does not fit, or turn, or work. If you force it you could break it."

Mom's intuition was evident in her unusual "spatial reasoning," as John describes it. One day he and his friend Dave Andrew were moving a heavy sofa from one small room, down a narrow hallway, and into another room. When it got stuck, Mom immediately visualized the answer and told them how it should be turned to get it through the narrow opening. We were amazed at how easy it was with her suggestion!

Cooking was a skill Mother learned from her mother and from experience over the years. I think the food Mom and her family had while growing up tasted especially delicious not only because their mother was such a good cook but also because they worked hard and got hungry. Today we are always looking for something fancy to eat because we are not really hungry and are bored with simple, even though delicious, foods.

Mom's favorite cookbook was the *Woman's Home Companion Cook Book*, published in 1945 by Garden City Publishing Company, Inc. She used this book to help teach us table settings, meal planning, nutrition, and other useful information. Besides her delicious Polish dishes, Mom made the best desserts. When making her doughnuts Mom would toss in leftover cereals, oatmeal, or cooked potatoes which would add dimension to the dough. She was a very good and innovative cook.

One day when we girls were little, Mother told us she would make us a large bowl of doughnuts before leaving for her rehearsal. When she returned home, she asked Dad why he looked so depressed. He said when he took a doughnut, one of us kids scolded, "Mom made those for *us*!"

Mom also made delicious cream puffs using the eggs from our ducks. For her Polish poppy seed cakes I remember Mom grinding the poppy seeds in an old-fashioned coffee grinder (the kind with a small drawer at the bottom). Cobblers were one of her specialties also. We picked and processed plums and apricots from our fruit trees. Her cobblers were never too sweet even though she topped them with her delicious *posipka*. Another favorite of ours was her homemade angel food cake with a topping of strawberry gelatin whipped up with fresh strawberries. This light, cool dessert was especially refreshing in the summer.

A few of the other dishes Mom taught us how to make were crispy fried chicken with mashed potatoes, steak with peppers and onions, pot roasts, soups, and stews. We had many tasty fish fries when Dad or other family members brought home lots of fresh-caught fish. (Dad taught me how to clean the fish, too!) Mom made great french fries and burgers as well as holiday ham and turkey dinners. Her potato pancakes and potato salad were the best! On hot summer days in Phoenix, we occasionally had a cool dinner of cottage cheese with peaches or with buttery noodles.

During the Depression and the war, Mom learned to cook foods I haven't eaten in a long time, like her delicious roasted beef tongue and kidney stew with potatoes, onions, and carrots. She cooked tasty liver and onions also. We still love to make her delicious chicken soup with dumplings, vermicelli, or wide egg noodles.

For family gatherings Mom made the best party punch with tea and fruit juices. One cousin always swore it was spiked, but it wasn't. A good cooking tip Mom taught me was that eggs and cheeses need to be cooked at low to medium heat.

Mom didn't drive, so she either walked to the store for her groceries or cooked whatever Dad brought home. Sometimes he would give her a break and surprise us with fried chicken or hamburgers from the local Dairy Queen. He also brought home root beer and vanilla ice cream to make root beer floats and often took us for an ice cream cone. (I remember the headliner of our car had a chocolate ice cream stain on it from one of us bouncing around as he was driving–before seatbelts were installed.)

Laundry was a never-ending chore in a family of seven. For a long time Mother did not have a clothes dryer. We girls learned to hang the clothes on the clothesline in the back yard.

My sisters and I remember if a storm was approaching, Mom would say "We have to batten down the hatches!" We had to close the windows, run outside to get the laundry off the clothesline, and bring in the swing cushions.

Helen's Girls Hanging Laundry

I can still remember Mom saying, "If they are not dirty, hang your clothes when you take them off so you can wear them again," and "If you wash your clothes less frequently the fabric stays newer-looking." Another tip was, "When washing something that has several pieces, wash *all* the pieces so they remain a uniform shade." Also, "Don't drop your clothes on the floor and walk on them–it breaks the fibers."

For pressing, Mother skillfully used a mangle. She actually preferred a mangle over an iron. I don't know how she did it with the mangle, but she could press Dad's postal uniforms with the shirt creases. She could even press the smallest ruffles with it! Mom also used pants stretchers to save time with Dad's pants. It was so hot in the summers with only evaporative cooling in our house that Mom said OK when Nancy asked her if she could put the sheets in the refrigerator!

Sewing and mending were valuable skills we first learned from Mother and Grandmother Karolina. We also learned sewing in school when girls all took "homemaking" classes. Sadly those classes are not required much any more in the public schools. My sisters and I loved making almost all our own clothes all the way through high school and college. Mom let us buy the best materials and wanted us to look nice. Important advice she gave us when sewing was "Quit when you are tired, or you will make mistakes." She said we could always work on it again the next day.

When the big crinolines were popular (those slips in the early '60s that made our skirts stand out almost horizontally), I would cut netting strips and sew for hours, ruffling the strips and stitching them together. One day in frustration Nancy said to me, "The house could be burning down, and you'd keep on sewing!" I don't know if she wanted the machine or what, but I remember being surprised at her comment!

The determined and loving spirit of our mother lived in Nancy, too, when we were in our teens. She surprised me one day with a beautiful, lined, two-piece green suit she had made for me to wear at an All State High School Chorus competition. I was amazed and flattered that she would do something like that for me. I didn't even know she was working on it until she handed it to me and asked me to try it on so she could measure for the hem. I will never forget how surprised and happy I felt that day.

When Nancy was in college, she was determined to make a new dress every weekend. I was impressed because she usually used a gorgeous upholstery fabric. The dresses were fabulous, and she never wore the same dress twice! She was voted the best dressed student of the year in the Arizona State University yearbook.

Frugality was a way of life for Mother. "Waste not, want not," was her motto. "You could feed a family on what you throw away," she used to tell me. She felt free to *use* things as needed, but she never wasted food, electricity, water, paper–anything.

Mother was sparing to herself and was generous to others. When she bought gifts, she bought practical items. She did not buy "showy" or trivial gifts. She did not try to match in value what someone else had given her. She also gave spontaneously and did not worry about buying gifts for the exact day of the occasion or holiday. She gave when she saw the perfect gift for someone, and it was usually high quality as well as practical—always practical. During the holidays she also kept a few items wrapped and ready to give to an unexpected guest.

I remember her simple gifts at Christmas time when we were kids. I liked the stocking stuffers the best—nail polish and lipstick from Avon (which she could shop for from home). I don't remember big things—maybe there weren't any, or perhaps they were not as important to me as the thoughtful little things.

Mother's gift of time was valued by many. When she could not help financially, she gave of her time, which often was a much more lasting gift. Throughout her life Mom took care of many family members and church friends—from infants to the aged. She was there to help as they were trying to work through life's problems or illnesses.

Even though she did not complain about it, Mother never got that diamond ring Dad had promised her. But when she saw the city lights at night from her desert property on the mountain, she said, "*That's* my diamond!"

Even though she was frugal, Mom always had a few new and stylish clothes and items of furniture. She knew how to take good care of them and kept them for a long time. She didn't mind when they were old or out of style. Having learned skills from her mother, she knew how to redesign and make over clothes that changed style or that no longer fit. She could turn a collar, add a gusset, take up the hem, remove the sleeves, add a ruffle, etc. When she couldn't make them over, she would say, "In another twenty years, these will be in style again." She was right!

As the years went by, Mother had trouble letting go of her old clothes and shoes. "Instead of shopping for more clothes, shop in your closet," she told me. I do now, and I save a lot of time and money. I find everything I need and more! Like the Bible says, I won't have room enough to contain all my blessings (Malachi 3:10b).

Mother was especially fond of keeping her old dishes, camping coffee pots, pans, and buckets. Raised as a coal-miner's daughter, she enjoyed keeping and reusing her old "treasures." We wanted her to have new stuff; we felt she deserved it. But she usually was not happy with new replacement items we bought, and we often had to return them. We wanted to take pride in our mom, so we weren't thinking about *her* desires, we were thinking about *ours*. I'm glad we eventually learned to respect her wishes and let her keep her old "stuff." We realized that she was not asking too much. One time, however, when Mother was widowed and living alone, we bought new items for the house and moved things around, trying to make life a little easier for her. She protested, saying, "There are too many changes in my house." Then on the phone she blithely told her sister, "I was ready for a change."

Even though Mom had trouble letting go of things, she *was* able to let go of "worry." I found a letter she wrote during World War II to one of her sisters. In it she wrote, "You have to let things go." She was writing in regards to problems they had no control over during the Depression and the war.

Recycling was natural for Mother and was another way for her to be frugal. She was artistic yet did not want to spend money on more art supplies. Instead, she made creative artifacts out of bits and pieces of paper she found around the house left over from our projects. She even used candy and gum wrappers! She covered oatmeal boxes and jars with colorful wrapping paper and used CD cases for photograph frames.

Health issues were always important to Mother. She always took good care of herself–her diet, teeth, skin, feet, hair, and nails. She said, "Your health is your most valuable possession." In the 1950s, with her interest in nutrition, Mom rode the bus to downtown Phoenix to Eichenaur's Health Food Store to buy vitamins, soy, and tiger's milk protein drinks, and studied nutritionist Adele Davis' books. In her later years she avidly watched "Dr. Cherry" on the TBN Television Network for his weekly nutrition lessons.

Mother knew that she was extremely sensitive to anesthetics. She could not even have Novocain for dental work. Her dentist was amazed that she could have her dental work done without it.

In the 1950s during childbirth, Mother pleaded with her doctors not to give her pain-killing drugs, but they did. They did not understand the side effects as well then as they do now. The drugs triggered a severe emotional reaction, and she had to be hospitalized. I remember my father crying as he talked to Aunt Frances on the phone. He asked her if she would come take care of us kids while Mom recovered. We were so blessed that the family was always there to help.

While Mom was in the hospital, the nurse gently tried to explain to her that she had a breakdown, Mother made everyone laugh when she said, "I didn't know I could afford one!" The doctor sent her home early because she started to get too involved with the other patients' problems instead of concentrating on her own, and they felt she wasn't getting enough rest.

Years later I asked Mother what helped her come out of her depression. She said it was the scripture, "Be still, and know that I am God" (Psalm 46:10a). Her doctor also gave her several pieces of advice which she shared with us. He said she needed to cry when she felt like it and not hold back the tears. He also told her not to force herself to do something. She remembered forcing herself to cook liver when she was pregnant. She knew liver would be good for her, and she normally loved it fried with onions. But when she was pregnant, she had an aversion to it and remembered the trauma she felt when she forced herself to cook it.

Mom also knew that chemicals cause cancer, so she used no pest-control chemicals in her home. Instead of chemicals she liked technology (as usual) and used the sound beepers which worked very well in her home.

Besides having a chemical-free home, Mom knew it was important to get plenty of sleep. Mom taught us the old adage, "An ounce of prevention is worth a pound of cure." When rested, work and play seem much more enjoyable. "Don't build up a sleep debt," she said. "If you lose one night's sleep, it takes two weeks to make it up."

At home Mom did not wake us except for school, church, or something important. She had us take naps in the summer when school was out to give herself a rest as well as for us to have "quiet time" even if we didn't sleep. On school nights we usually went to our rooms at 7:00 p.m. and were up early in the morning. She believed children needed ten hours of sleep or rest daily. I still remember Mom covered us up on cold nights as we slept and in the early morning hours, as her mother must have done. I didn't even know I was cold until she covered me, and I still remember how warm it felt.

One thing Mother realized as she got older was that she should not have been sleeping on the side of her face. I remember she met me at the front door one day and said, "Look at these lines. I should not have been sleeping on my face!"

After learning of the dangers of too much sun, Mom always wore a hat to prevent skin problems. One of her sisters made fun of her and her hats, but later admitted, "You were right, Helen." One brother and one sister had to have skin cancer removed from their faces.

Regarding our teeth, Mom taught us, "Be true to your teeth, and they won't be false to you."

When Mom was having trouble with her vision, she thought that letters she received in the mail were just copied too light. After a checkup it was determined she needed to have cataracts removed. After the surgery, she said with tears in her eyes, "It's like when I was baptized—everything looks new!"

Safety was one of my mother's main concerns. She always wanted the children to be carefully watched. She said "Remember, safety first!" as we went off to baby sit. I guess she knew of dangers we couldn't even imagine.

For safety when we were young, Mom stopped using her favorite wringer washing machine. She saw our childish fascination with it, and she did not want to take a chance on one of us getting hurt. Her mother Karolina had almost caught her long hair in a wringer, and her brother had mashed his finger in the gears. It was just too risky with little ones around.

When her granddaughter, Christine, came to visit as an adult she said, "Grandma, I have a funny feeling as I walk around in your house." Mom said, "That is because when I took care of you, I always held you and watched over you. I never let you just run around unsupervised. This house was not child safe at that time."

Other good advice was given to us by Mother over the years. A few of her tips include the following:

"Try to be happy to make those around you happy."

"Haste makes waste."

"Practice makes perfect."

"Read the paper, or at least scan it every day."

"Don't leave without saying good-bye."

"Don't make important decisions when you are tired or angry."

"Try three times before asking for help." (to avoid "learned helplessness")

"Always feed the family. Don't use food as leverage when you are angry. There is a better chance of resolving problems when we are not hungry."

There were times I thought Mother was too patient. But now I appreciate the fact that she took the time to teach us, and our family stayed intact even through tough times. This could only have been done with her love and quiet, determined, and faithful spirit.

Mother's patience was often observed in her countenance. I remember the way she looked at me at times when she was listening to me. She would cock her head slightly, look straight into my eyes, and listen. I could see the "wheels turning," and I felt she was truly considering what I was saying. Then she would respond with her wonderful intuition and wisdom.

Parenting patience with adult children is also needed at times. One day when I was frustrated by my children, I asked my mother, "Why do I have to teach them the same things over and over?" She said, "You will never be finished teaching them." I had never considered that idea before, but now I can see that she was right.

As young adults, when we girls were marrying or divorcing and Mom disagreed with us over something, she never tried to force her will on us. She told us her opinion, but she let us know it was our decision. So after she had been widowed for three years, and we didn't want her to marry a man she had only known for five weeks, she looked us straight in the eye and said, "You girls made your mistakes, and I'll make mine." What could we say?

Later she learned, again, that she could not put her trust in people. This husband tried to set up numerous conflicts between Mother and her family members. When I pointed out to her that he was trying to "divide and conquer," she recognized it and refused to allow it to happen. When he divorced her for not selling her property to put him into business, she was heartbroken.

Years earlier when I had been divorced, Mom had said, "There is something you could have done to save your marriage." Now, however, she could see that it is not always possible to save a marriage, or the price could be one we did not want to pay.

Toward the end of her life Mother still had wonderful words of advice. "After you make a decision, stick with it. Don't keep changing your mind and undoing work that has already been done." When I wanted to interview for a job teaching at the University of Phoenix, she said, "Just keep the job you've got." That was good advice. I immediately felt a sense of relief. After thirty-five years of teaching in Scottsdale at that time, why should I start a new job? I'm thankful for all of her good advice over the years.

A great agreement regarding invitations between us and our widowed mother was appreciated by all of us. We felt we were being neglectful if we did not invite her to go everywhere with us. And she felt that if she declined an invitation we would not ask her again. So I told her, "Let's agree that we could feel free to invite you, and that you could feel free to say no." She expressed her appreciation many times for that agreement during the last several years of her life.

When her health was failing fast, I tried to convince Mother to go to the doctor, but she did not want to go. She had what is called "the white coat syndrome." She hated to go to the doctors and that caused her blood pressure to go sky high. With her determined spirit still very strong, she said, "Let me live the last half hour of my life the way I want to!" So I did. Since she never forced us, we never forced her.

I do not try to force my will on my adult children today. I may give my advice, but I let them make their choices and hope they let me make mine when I'm in their care some day. Interesting, isn't it–the relationship between parent and child. "What goes around comes around," as they say.

15

Mom 2000-2001

For to me, to live is Christ and to die is gain.
Philippians 1:21

"**I had an interesting and full life,**" Mom told me one day. "I worked hard, I had fun, and I did what I wanted. Now I just want to rest."

"You deserve to rest!" I replied. Mom said her mind never felt any older than eighteen, but her body was wearing out. But she had succeeded in "growing old gracefully." She had long since stopped singing in the symphonic choir and the church choir before she could no longer sing beautifully.

Mother had always taken good care of us, and as we got older, she let us take over gradually and learn to care and do things for her. When she asked her step-grandson to make coffee for her, he asked why. She responded, "So that when I'm old, you'll know how."

Precious moments were shared with individuals or with small groups of people as Mom got older. She had always loved traveling, camping, and visiting family members, but she became more comfortable at home over the years. On rare occasions Mom and her sisters would spend the night at each other's homes. I remember when Aunt Agnes came over to Mom's house and they had a "sleep over" (as the kids call it) for eleven days!

As it got more difficult to get out, she and her friends and family talked on the phone more often. They called each other to watch a certain TV show or just chatted. Mom used to call me occasionally to watch a program she thought was interesting. It sometimes irritated me then, but I miss those calls now.

For the last two years of her life, Mother left her home only once. She was weakened with congestive heart failure, diabetes, high blood pressure, and high cholesterol. She was afraid that if she pushed herself, she might have a stroke.

That one last trip out of her house was when she came over to my house to vote on the Internet in November of 2000. She had missed the cut-off for her mail-in ballot, and (even though we supported opposing parties) I told her she could vote on the computer. "Really?" she perked up. And being the technology lover that she was, she said, "OK!" Her brother Joe and I helped her make it over to my house. My husband Jesse helped her vote and printed out her certificate for being one of the first ever to vote online! She was so happy to be able to do that. She always took pride in voting. She knew many had paid the price for that privilege.

While housebound and bedridden, Mom loved to watch TV. She was able to watch some of the World War II movies that she could not watch until long after Dad died. She loved the old black and white romance and mystery movies of her youth. When she was young, she had been told she looked like movie stars Paulette Goddard and Myrna Loy. Mom especially enjoyed the musicals filled with singing and dancing.

Some of her favorite more recent programs were *M.A.S.H.*, *Frazier*, *Mayberry*, *Dr. Cherry*, and *Melody Mountain*. When I asked what her favorite soap opera was she thought a moment and then replied, "I think it is called, *Are These My Children?*" We all had a good laugh over that one!

Mother also loved to watch the Arizona Diamondbacks play baseball on TV. She and Uncle Otto called each other to ask, "Are you watching the game?" One day as her health was failing, she asked me weakly, "I don't want to watch the game, but could you put the TV on and just tell me what the score is?"

I remember many pleasant times and conversations with my mother. We laughed and laughed so much. She told my sister Nancy, "If I had my 'd'ruthers,' I would love to live in a tree-filled park, but that would not be 'acceptable' to my family." Mom's last goal was to sit outside and enjoy her yard. At that point she could only look out the window and see how green the grass was. She commented on how nice John kept it up.

Mom's neighbor Amy knew Mom was becoming hard of hearing because the TV gradually got louder and louder. She knew something was wrong when the TV went quiet.

Mom began to talk to us about her dreams. She saw her sisters, and she cried when she talked of seeing her mother. She dreamed of dancing with Dad and he had both arms—no longer a war amputee. She dreamed of his mother and father also.

A song she wanted to hear again which reminded her of West Virginia was John Denver's "Country Roads." "Country roads, take me home to the place I belong, West Virginia mountain momma take me home country roads."

Mom made us promise her that we would let her live out the rest of her days in her own home, and we did. One time she said, "I'm so sorry you have to work so hard to take care of me, Jimmie Lou."

I replied, "Mom, did you mind taking care of your mother?"

"No," she replied softly.

"And I don't mind taking care of you!" I assured her.

For the last few years of her life I washed Mom's long, beautiful, silky, silver-gray hair. She sat in a chair with her back to the sink, and I used a hair-washing tray to catch most of the water. (She laughed when I accidentally let water run down her back!) Then I dried it, combed it, and braided it, to keep it from getting tangled. When we wanted to cut it, she insisted on keeping it long because she had promised her mother she would let it grow long.

Mother tried to be strong for as long as she could. She refused to use a walker or a wheelchair even though I had them handy for her. "Those are for old people," she said.

"Jimmie Lou, take care of your health." This was the last advice she ever gave to me.

"Have the poor been taken care of?" Mother asked me as I wrote out checks for her. If someone asked for a handout on the street, Mom taught us, "Buy him a meal, but don't give cash because it will probably be spent on alcohol." She always gave to food banks and organizations which helped the needy. One of her favorites was still the Christian Appalachian Project which helps those she still identified with from her childhood in West Virginia.

As the days passed, Mom tried hard to remember words to songs that would help her release her hold on this earth. One was a phrase from the hymn, "Rock of Ages, Cleft For Me"–"In my hands no price I bring, simply to Thy cross I cling." Several comforting scriptures were "Death has been swallowed up in victory!" (I Corinthians 15:54b), and "To live is Christ and to die is gain" (Philippians 1:21). She also tried to recall a phrase from the "Hail Mary," a Catholic prayer she had memorized long ago as a child, "...pray for us sinners, now and at the hour of our death."

During the morning of September 11, 2001, after the terrorist attacks on the Twin Towers in New York, the Pentagon, and the hijacked plane in Pennsylvania, I went over to Mother's house early before she could see or hear about the attacks. When I got there, Mom told me she had awakened in the night. She said she had "a strong feeling–like the world was coming to an end." Even though bedridden she had sat up, smoothed out her bed sheets, folded the towels she had lying around her, and organized her belongings that were within reach of her bed. Once again her intuitive spirit had awakened her with the feeling that something was about to happen. So I did tune in her TV to watch what she already sensed was happening. For many, the world did come to an end that day.

Mom had always told us she wanted to be in her home when she died. On October 23, 2001, we had to take her to hospice care. "Just for a few days," we promised her. One of the most beautiful moments while she was in the wonderful care of Hospice of the Valley was when a volunteer harpist came into her room and played a few songs. Mother loved it. The woman asked her if she had a request, and Mom said, "Do you know 'Only a Rose'?" Amazingly, the harpist did know this song from *The Vagabond King* and played it while Mother sang with her clear, beautiful voice:

> "Only a rose I give you,
> Only a song dying away,

Only a smile to keep in memory,
Until we meet another day!"

On another day as I was saying good-bye to Mother to go run some errands, she squeezed my hands very tightly. I got the feeling she didn't want to let go. Now I wish I had held her hands a little longer that day.

After one week in a hospice care facility we brought her home on October 30. She asked me, "Am I at home?" I said, "Yes, Mom. See, on the shelf are the dolls your mother made. Yes, you are at home," I reassured her.

My brother John had told me that if she talks to other people in the room when it seems no one is there, she is talking to angels. That is exactly what happened the day Mother died. I remember she softly spoke with her eyes closed. I could see she was drifting away and had to ask, louder than usual, "What did you say, Mom?" She said softly, "No more medicine." I believe she was talking with the angels. A little while later she murmured, "The colors are pretty." I believe she was describing the unimaginable colors of Heaven. Heaven was being revealed to her at that very moment! Most people don't usually take a trip alone. If they do, they wish they could share the best experiences with someone. I believe Mother was being escorted into Heaven by angels or by Jesus Himself!

I was by her side on November 3, 2001, when Mother took her last earthly breath. She was in her home, just as she had wished. My sisters and brothers were all there, and we gathered around her bed. Through our tears we sang hymns, giving thanks to God that she was not dead but was now living in eternity with Jesus!

꙳

We all miss Mom so much. She always understood us. She always was patient with us. She always encouraged us and made us laugh. We now have to "take the baton"–her spirit of determination, love, and faith–and "run with it." We must "pass it on" by sharing with each other and with generations to follow.

As I drive home from work I still want to stop by and see her. Then I remember–she's not there. At other times I want to call her to ask her something. I want to tell her or show her something I think she will enjoy. And she's not there. But then I realize her spirit is in the car with me! Her spirit lives on in eternity where there is no past and no future but, eternally, "the present." Her spirit lives in me!

My mother Helen and Grandmother Karolina honored God and blessed all they knew with their lives and love. Every day I have left on this earth I want to honor them. God has promised to bless those who honor their parents. "Honor your father and mother—which is the first commandment with a promise—that it may go well with you and that you may enjoy long life on the earth" (Ephesians 6:2-3).

A very strange thing occurred on the day my mother died. The Arizona Diamondbacks were winning The 2001 World Series against the New York Yankees, scoring numerous runs in a matter of minutes. Strangely, on the other side of the country in Connecticut my sister Sally's mother-in-law, Carolyn Nardozzi, also died that same day. Later I wondered if the two of them were up to something. They both loved to watch baseball, and they were rooting for opposing teams . . . Hmm . . . . I wonder if they just wanted better seats to watch this exciting game before going off to Heaven—together!

16

Memories from Cousins and Friends

*One generation shall praise Thy works to another,
And shall declare Thy mighty acts. Psalm 145:4 (KJ)*

Cousins and friends have shared with me a few of the special moments they remember about my grandmother Karolina, her children and their friends, and my parents, Helen and Jim, over the years. They remember the spirit of determination, faith, and love expressed through their lives. Some of my brothers, sisters, cousins, and I are renewing our appreciation for the values of our foundations in God, in our grandparents, and in our parents. We now share these values with our children, grandchildren, and the generations to follow.

Cousin Audrey Ann remembers when she was a little girl she spent many days with her grandmother Karolina in Chicago. Karolina took her to the park where they watched the people, young and old, singles and couples, and parties on occasion. Sometimes she went with her mother Verna to the Aragon Ballroom to dance and drink soda. At home Karolina cut thick slices of rye bread at an angle to get a lot of golden crust, covered them with butter, and served them with coffee (with a lot of milk in it for little Audrey Ann!). Grandma told her not to mention the coffee to her mother!

Audrey also remembers when she was a young girl, how her Grabiec aunts and uncles worked in Chicago, brought home their money, and put it on the table for their mother. She saw this as a "privilege" of being an adult and could hardly wait to get a job so she could give the money to her mother. When she was old enough and got a job, she, too, gave the money to her mother and felt pride in being a functioning member of her family. She then asked her mother for money to buy a skirt or whatever else she needed.

Audrey remembers how her Aunt Helen's energy and enthusiasm excited her as a young girl growing up in Chicago. Audrey went with Helen to the Chicago Theater, describing it as "beautiful with elegant velvet and gold trim and large staircases." She remembers enjoying movies and live performances by stars like Bob Hope and Red Skelton. Audrey remembers meeting Mom's music director, Lois Albright, in Chicago and her performing in musicals there.

Audrey wanted to study voice and perform in musicals like her Aunt Helen, but her parents wanted her to study classical music. So, with the conflict of opinion on musical styles, she did neither. When Audrey's family moved to Phoenix, Mom knew Audrey was broken-hearted by being uprooted from her senior high school friends. Mom told Audrey, "Phoenix is nothing like Chicago for theater, but it is still good here." Mom encouraged her to audition for the lead part as "Julie" in *Carousel*, but by that time Audrey had lost her desire to sing. Mom sensed her disappointment and did not force her. She just wanted her to think about it.

When Audrey became engaged at a young age, Mom wanted her to carefully think that through also. She told Audrey that marriage was not always a "bed of roses" or "peaches and cream."

My cousins Carole Jane and Audrey remember their 1944 trip to visit Galloway with their mothers, Frances and Verna, Karolina's twins. (They also remember getting lice in their hair on the train! Their mothers had to use kerosene to delouse them!)

Carole Jane has fond memories of Grandmother Karolina and my parents, Helen and Jim. One favorite is Grandma playing "This Little Piggy" with her in Polish. Carole describes my mother and father as having been "pioneers" in Arizona. Carole's husband, Fred Spencer, remembers my dad and liked him very much. He remembers how he enjoyed sitting under the ramada my dad built on our desert property, just enjoying a beer, pleasant conversation, and the quiet desert.

Years later in 1998 Carole Jane remembers my mother singing "Ave Maria" with her in Latin at Frances' funeral reception. Mother still had a beautiful voice at age seventy-nine.

Cousin Richard remembers the fun he had when the Grabiecs' good friend Willie Nemeth took him canoeing at age five at the Encanto Park Lagoon in Phoenix. Many years later Richard's son, Gary, remembers when he was five and Willie visited his Grandmother Frances in Bartonville, Illinois. Little Gary walked around in Willie's gigantic shoes and later said, "They were the biggest shoes I had ever seen!"

Richard remembers my mom and dad were like his own family. "Your folks were good to me," he remembers. In the winters he and his mother, Mom's sister Frances, came out to visit, and my parents took him on trips around Arizona in the late 1940s. He remembers going horseback riding with my mother at Weldon Stables near South Mountain. He said, "Let's ride over to those mountains." She said, "OK, but we only have the horses for two hours." He remembers riding on and on and never getting near the mountains. He learned how deceiving distances can be! But he probably thought that if they had ridden faster they could have made it. "You ride like a girl!" he had told her.

After riding, Richard recalls stopping at the old store "made of stones" where he was excited to see a Gila monster on a rock outside the door. He also remembers climbing Squaw Peak, now known as Piestewa Peak, when there was no trail and no one else climbing. He went up the west side—straight up, he remembers. He is amazed at the thousands of climbers there today, hiking the well-worn trail which begins on the southeast side.

As the oldest grandson, Richard was given one of Grandmother Karolina's old *pierzynas* stuffed with chicken and goose down feathers. He believes this is one of those she brought with her from Czechoslovakia in 1913. Richard's family had used it to keep warm on cold days in Illinois. He is preserving it as a family treasure.

Even though she did not live nearby, Cousin Marilyn remembers Grandma Karolina and my mother. At age four Marilyn came to Phoenix on the train with her mother, Betty. She remembers Grandma combing her hair while they were sitting on Grandma's door stoop. She also remembers riding in the desert in a pickup truck and sitting on Grandma's lap on the way to tour the Blue Bird Mine in Goldfield, Arizona not far from the Superstition Mountains.

Visit to Blue Bird Mine

When Marilyn was about nine or ten, she remembers her Aunt Helen came to visit in Ohio and took Marilyn to the Bach Festival at Baldwin Wallace College. It was held outdoors on a beautiful spring day, and Marilyn remembers how she loved experiencing classical music and a full orchestra for the first time! Marilyn's last memory of Grandma Karolina is when she visited their new home on Alexander Road in Bedford, Ohio, in the early 1950s.

Cousin Carolyn is named after our Grandmother Karolina and was about four when she knew her Grabiec grandparents. She only remembers Grandma saying, "Co b͵edzie, co b͵edzie (What will be, will be)." Carolyn remembers the one time she met her grandfather Frank Sr. She was riding in the car with him, and he completely ignored her. She remembers thinking, "He doesn't like me."

Cousin Marlene remembers how my mother used to call for me in her operatic soprano voice–"Jimmie Loo-oooo!"–with a rise and then a drop, musically, like singing an ascending fifth step to a descending third.

Cousin Hayden Lee remembers meeting Mother for the first time when Dad brought her to Chickasha, Oklahoma, to meet his parents. He remembers how pretty she was and what a good couple they made. He also recalls, years later when Dad returned from the hospital with war injuries, how Mom tried to be cheerful and upbeat to keep his spirits up.

When Hayden and his mother, Jessie (Dad's sister), lived in Phoenix for a while, Hayden remembers how cheerful, sweet and gracious my mother was to him and his mother. He remembers her beautiful voice as she played the piano and sang. He especially remembers the delicious spaghetti and salads she served and all of us piling into the car and going to the drive-in theater.

Friends also remind me of wonderful times shared with Mom over the years in Phoenix. Susan and her parents were our neighbors for more than thirty years. Susan remembers my mother very well. "I have fond memories of how your mother loved my mother and father." Susan's mother enjoyed Mom's cooking and came over to visit often. From her house next door Susan remembers hearing Mother singing and vocalizing. When her own little step-daughter, Jennifer, was sick, Susan remembers how sweet Mother had been to make some soup for her.

Susan also remembers my Grandmother Karolina. She remembers us sitting around the table as children, talking and eating farina, which my mother cooked often for us when we were young. I still think of my mother when I make farina today. It is one of my family's favorite breakfasts.

My friend Brenda told me she remembers the sound of my Mom's voice. Mom and Brenda's dad, Rod, had both lost their life-long spouses, so we decided to take them with us on a trip to Tucson for a ball game. Mom animatedly talked during the entire drive to Tucson. She was so happy to have his undivided attention. The funny thing about it is that Brenda's dad was hard of hearing and probably heard only a fraction of what she said! But they sure had a good time, anyway!

Part Five: Her Spirit Lives

17

Her Spirit Lives On in Us

*I thought about the former days, the years of long ago;
I remembered my songs in the night. Psalm 77:5-6a*

I'm thankful for the spirit of determination, love, and faith that lived in my grandmother, Karolina, and my mother, Helen. I'm thankful for their love of America, for their creativity, their love of music, their optimism, and their willingness to let God be God in their lives.

I'm also thankful that their spirit lives on in me and my sisters and brothers. I am energized in all I do as a wife, mother, homemaker, teacher, researcher, gardener, world traveler, and writer. My husband, **Jesse**, a U. S. Army veteran, and our children, Liz and Zac, also have been touched by my mother's loving spirit and love of life.

Like my parents and grandparents, I love and appreciate America. In 1963 I left for eight weeks when I sang for the U. S. Armed Forces in Germany and France with the YMCA

1998 The Watson Family

Youth Chorus. I enjoyed traveling, but I saw few smiles and there seemed to be a spirit of hopelessness at the time I traveled in the mid '60s. Living outside of the United States made me really appreciate America for the first time, and I was happy to get back to "one nation under God."

An honor for me occurred that same year when I was crowned the first Miss Polonia at the Pulaski Club in Phoenix. For the competition I sang Chopin's "*Zyczenie*" ("The Maiden's Wish") in Polish, with the expert coaching of Harriet Alexander. I consider holding this title a great privilege in memory of my Polish mother and grandparents.

1963 First Miss Polonia in Phoenix

When I was in college and my brothers were little, I enjoyed watching them develop our mother's spirit of creativity and improvisation. Instead of buying toys, I collected boxes of "stuff" they could build with—scraps which would usually be thrown in the trash—bottle tops, pieces of wire, Styrofoam, plastic crates, small boxes, plastic, metal, cardboard, foil, etc. To the box I added paper plates, tape, glue, scissors, and string. With these they could make things using their own creative ideas. They loved it! They made miniature buildings, model houses with furniture, flying saucers with stairs of folded strips of paper, and other creative objects. Like our mother with her "sardine can toys," they felt a sense of pride and accomplishment in using their imagination and constructing interesting toys on their own.

Today Mother's love of music lives on in me. I am uplifted by the beautiful and inspiring Christian music on Family Life Radio KFLR. I have many "favorite" songs including "Sometimes By Step" by the late Rich Mullins,

"I Can't Live a Day Without You" by Avalon, "The Power of Your Love" by Maranatha with Matthew Ward, and "Legacy" by Nichole Nordeman. Old hymns of inspiration and truth which I learned as a child in church also come to mind and inspire me. Three of my many favorites are "Living for Jesus," "Trust and Obey," and "What a Friend We Have in Jesus."

I also share in my mother's spirit of optimism and faith. I have learned to look for the bright side of a situation, and if I can't find one, to trust God with it. A book that inspires me daily is *Streams in the Desert* by L. B. Cowman. I rely on the commands and promises of God to be anxious for nothing, but by prayer and thanksgiving let my requests be made known to Him. And the peace which surpasses all comprehension shall guard my heart and mind in Christ Jesus (Philippians 4:6-7). Wow, what a promise!

Having seen the love that strengthened their lives, I pray that I, too, will decrease and that He will increase in my life (John 3:30 KJ). And I must pray *believing* (James 1:6)! His Word is *living* and is "a lamp to my feet and a light for my path" (Psalm 119:105). In it he promises me "abundant life" (John 10:10 KJ), which I have!

Karolina's spirit of determination, love, and faith also lives on in my sisters and brothers in many unique ways. We each live our own lives, but we know we are there for each other. When we have a word of advice, we give it simply, privately, and without drama or gossip. We call or visit occasionally but also give each other our "space."

Nancy, my sister, is a mother and an inspired artist, sculptor, painter, photographer, film maker, researcher, writer, gardener, seamstress, and cook. I appreciate her love and wisdom. I can see the spirit of Karolina living on in her today as well as in her son, Nick.

"We are always at a point in life where we have the most lessons to learn," Nancy believes. One of her favorite scriptures is Romans 8:28, "We know that in all things God works for the good of those who love Him, who have been called according to His purpose." This verse, written in the present tense, affirms the fact that He is working *right now* on our behalf.

1974 Nancy and Nick

When Mom was ill and becoming weaker, I shared with Nancy my fears of what might happen next regarding her care. Nancy taught me not to worry about what will happen next. She reminded me that in Matthew 6:34, Jesus said, "Do not worry about tomorrow, for tomorrow will worry about itself. Each day has enough troubles of its own." She said, "Just take the next step, but don't worry about tomorrow." I took her advice, stopped worrying, and the problems I feared never materialized. Nancy taught me to live the present moment. And she is right—all of eternity is existing in "the present!"

Nancy is now the emotional leader of our family. She inherited this role when our precious mother died. I call Nancy when I need moral support or a bit of advice. Nancy has Grandmother Karolina's quiet manner and calm countenance. I rarely see her angry. Her words of wisdom calm and comfort me. When I feel discouraged, she reminds me that Mom's spirit of love is still with us.

Besides her faith that God is in control, Nancy believes in taking the "middle path"—all things in moderation. She has shared with me some of her other tips for success also. She accomplishes much in her life because she makes plans, paces herself, and tries to do at least one thing on each project every day. Another tip she gave me is when she has a question while reading, writing, or researching, she looks up the answer right away so she doesn't forget to look it up later, never learning the answer. She also advises that to work more efficiently, take a ten-minute break every hour.

"**Sally** is the only grandchild I didn't have to spank," Grandmother Karolina said of my sister Sally. She is a beautiful mother, grandmother, homemaker, singer, artist, calligrapher, baker, writer, seamstress, and world traveler.

Sally's sensitive, loving, and faithful spirit is evident in the way she gives of her time and talents to the family, to her friends, and to her church. She has an "I can help!" attitude. She trusts God and is thankful for her blessings.

With her spirit of determination Sally overcomes seemingly insurmountable tasks by "baby-stepping" to accomplish her goals. We like to laugh about "getting our 'duck' in a row!"

1987 The Nardozzi Family

Sally and I love to travel, as did our mother and grandmother. Maybe that is why at the age of four, Sally wanted to run away. She packed her tiny straw suitcase with her favorite items—her ballet slippers and her skate key. She walked all the way to the edge of the driveway, sat down on her suitcase, and wondered who was going to drive her! We were always there to rescue her. And we've been traveling ever since—even today.

While visiting the quaint town of Oak Creek, Colorado, we got to experience the place where our Grandfather Frank lived out the last years of his life. We especially enjoyed visiting with Peter Yurich, the "town historian," over the Labor Day weekend.

Today Sally practices the motto, "Bloom where you're planted." (And she also loves gardening!) Open to His leading, she prays "Whatever it is you have for me today, Lord, don't let me miss it!"

Sally and her husband **Bob** enjoy singing in their church choir and working in their creative catering business, Leigh and Nardozzi Caterers and Bakery in Gloucester Point, Virginia. They are the proud parents of three—Christine, Jenny, and Jeremy. They are also the grandparents of four blessed children who have the spirit of Grandmother Karolina living in them—her fifth generation!

My brothers did not have the privilege of knowing Grandmother Karolina, but they did see her spirit of determination, love, and faith living in our mother. Through this book I share with them, and with the rest of the world, the grandmother we knew and loved so much.

Herb fulfilled our parents' dream for a boy. From an early age Karolina's spirit of determination was apparent in him. Before he could even walk, he figured out how to "escape" from his crib by lying on his stomach, backing up to the crib bars, stretching one foot at a time over the top, pulling himself up, dropping himself down the outside edge, and crawling away!

Herb is gifted, inventive, adventurous, and sensitive. He is a United States Army veteran, world traveler, speaker, researcher, and landscaper, and he likes to hike and camp.

In his youth Herb developed Mother's love of technology. He was fascinated with electronics, and he read books about it like children read novels. At age fifteen Herb took the Certified Electronics Technician (CET) test, finishing first that day. He worked with Uncle Frank at his shop, Dyna Tronics, while receiving high school credit since he already knew the information being taught his senior year. He quickly became the youngest Certified Electronics Technician ever in the state of Arizona. Today Herb is working on the cutting edge of alternative fuel technology development.

Herb travels all over the United States and the world, teaching and learning the latest technological advances. In Prescott, Arizona, he has coordinated the development of the largest solar collector of its type in the world.

Herb's spirit of love was shared with the family of our niece's Hungarian husband when they visited from Hungary. His determined spirit worked patiently, overcoming the language barrier and sharing his interest in their lives and their visit.

John has the intuitive and artistic talents of our mother and grandmother. Inspired by our mother's talent and love of music, he has developed his talents by singing, performing, and directing. He is also gifted in the areas of design and architecture. John loves traveling the world, landscaping, gardening, cooking and writing.

In the seventh grade John recovered a wing chair for our mother. Even though the fabric was $50 a yard, she bought what he wanted. And he did a professional job of it! Later she told him, "You told me you could do it. And I knew that if you said you could do it, you would." For an eighth grade science project John designed a circular model home. He later constructed a light fixture out of tin cans for his bedroom ceiling. Like our mother, John also loves technology. He has a robot vacuum cleaner and even magnetizes his drinking water!

John did not know Grandmother Karolina, but her spirit of determination that lived in our mother now lives on in him. "Grandma had glimpses of what was possible," he said regarding her leaving Czechoslovakia. "And the alternatives in Europe at that time were dismal if not fatal. Her story is about rising above adversity. She knew that if she continued doing what was right—if she took care of her children and took responsibility for her obligations—everything would work out." As he thinks about our parents, he surmises, "Our parents had to Americanize us, but this book trumpets our ethnicity!"

Regarding education, John remembers that, with Mother's confidence in us, she never discussed our going to college. She didn't discourage us nor did she presume we were going. He believes that the presupposition about going or not going to college can be a huge deterrent to success. It can also be a deterrent to openness toward other opportunities of which one could take advantage. Mom gave us permission to be ourselves. When he asked her opinion about his studying music and performing, she said, "Do it now while you are young, or you never will." Today John has a career in both singing and home design as inspired by our mother.

One of John's favorite quotes is, "A word aptly spoken is like apples of gold in settings of silver" (Proverbs 25:11). Following his resolution of a personal difficulty, Mother once told him, "All of my life I have thought that you were one of the most wonderful people I have ever met, and I was amazed that you were my son. There is absolutely nothing I would ever change about you." Some people wait their whole life for a parent to tell them this!

When he was "bad," however, Mom simply said, "The guilty flee when none pursue" (Proverbs 28:1).

John loves to cook and recalls Mom's perplexing reply when he asked her for a recipe for crepes. She said, "Use eggs, flour and milk." "How much of each?" he asked. "You'll know when it looks right," was her answer!

With our mother's and grandmother's spirit of love, John continually gives of himself and cares for his family and friends. Like Karolina's supporting her brother Rudy's move from Czechoslovakia to America, John helped "launch" our niece Jenny when she wanted to go to college far away in Hawaii. Unity and support have always been a priority in our family.

Mother once told John she would never sell her home, saying, "It is important for you to always feel you have a home to come home to." Now he owns her home, and he considers it a privilege to live there and care for it and the yard she loved so much.

Vivid visions and dreams of our mother and father come to John ever since they passed into eternity. One he calls "A Glimpse of the Future."

> "Mom and Dad are standing in the front yard under the silk oak tree. They both appear to be around twenty-eight and are a tremendously handsome couple. He's in gray wool dress pants, starched white shirt, and wide geometric tie. Mom is in a gray wool calf-length pencil skirt and a white silk blouse. Soft curls frame her face, and her hair is pulled back into a chignon. Dad has both arms and is looking at a little dog on the end of a leash. He is relaxed and happy . . . . Mom is just gazing at Dad, and I can feel how much she loves him."

John's favorite vision follows:

> "Two huge double doors open inward, revealing a glimpse of the interior of a gigantic room. Mom is about twenty-eight and is backing into the room, smiling. She is barefoot, dressed in a flowing white, floor-length gown, as alluring as a goddess

but not at all provocative. The walls of the room are covered in layer after layer of white silk, drawn back by gold cords. I can feel the luxuriousness of the white carpet under her feet. She says, laughingly, '*This* is where I live now!'"

~

Helen, Then and Now!

Karolina and Helen knew that God gives us each a unique spirit. They also knew that characteristics can be fostered, like Karolina's quiet spirit of determination and courage as well as love for family and friends. To endure the unforeseen problems in life they believed in the One who created all things. They knew He would be there through them all. If we share in this faith and trust Him every moment of every day with the little things as well as the big things, we will not need to fear. God has not given us the spirit of fear, but of power, and of love, and of a sound mind (2 Timothy 1:7 KJ).

We need to be determined in fostering a spirit of forgiveness with present and future generations. By forgiving, we can be forgiven. We can start fresh every day with no grudges to hinder our prayers to the One who made us and lives in us (Matthew 6:15).

The windows of Heaven were opened to me by the working of God's spirit through my grandmother and mother. He is still living and working through those who are willing to accept His free gift of the water of life (Revelation 22:17). He is only a whispered prayer away!

18

The Fourth and Fifth Generations

I have no greater joy than to hear that my children are walking in the truth. 3 John 4

The fourth and fifth generations of Karolina's family now have the awesome responsibility of sharing her love, faith, and determination with future generations.

As Jonas Salk said, it is important to give children roots and wings. I gave my children "roots" in a foundation of truth so they would have something to choose from when "using their wings" and making choices in their lives. Did I teach them what they need to know? Will they remember what I taught them? Like my grandmother and mother before me, I trust God with those answers.

I know our children are born with their own God-given talents and temperament. Yet much of who they are and become is nurtured by experiences within the family.

My children belong to their great-grandmother Karolina's fourth generation. They did not know her, but they did know their Grandmother Helen.

My daughter **Elizabeth Anne** was born May 3, 1979. Liz remembers her grandmother's love, her sense of humor, and the funny things she did. On our trips to Dewey to visit her Aunt Nancy, her grandmother always toted several bags of sweaters, snacks, and water for the short one and one-half-hour drive.

She always had candy in her purse in case someone had a "low sugar" headache or just wanted something sweet.

Liz has her great-grandparents' love of music, and she played the violin for eight years. She is creative and artistic and has her great-grandparents' determined and courageous spirit of adventure. After visiting Spain, Canada, and Mexico as a teen she is now teaching for the U. S. Department of Defense in South Korea and travels with her husband **Eric** to countries around the world. Eric has a degree in psychology and is now a graduate student in counseling. He teaches and works as a behavior specialist with Elizabeth in the D.O.D. American Schools.

2004 Liz and Eric Eklund

I remember the day Liz and Eric were leaving for South Korea. As we walked to the car, Liz looked at me with a hesitant smile and said, "Well, here I go!" She and I were experiencing the fear of the unknown at that moment. Was this a small taste of the apprehension which Karolina and her mother, Mary, felt in 1913 as Karolina left Czechoslovakia for America?

My son **Zachary Andrew** was born October 8, 1981. Zac quietly describes his relationship with his grandmother Helen as "personal." They had a special bond—it was just between the two of them. Zac shares her spirit of determination—he knows what he wants and goes after it until he gets it. (When he wants me to do something, he quietly stares at me with that calm, quiet, determined look until I respond!) He also has his grandmother's love of music, dance, and performing. He is artistic and creative in style and design, and his hair design was published on the cover of the October 1-7, 2003, edition of *College Times Magazine* even before he graduated from cosmetology school.

Nick Quade, my sister Nancy's son, born December 28, 1972, exhibits the spirit of determination and love of family which his great-grandmother Karolina and grandmother Helen felt. He is a successful businessman and loves music and family get-togethers. Nick believes he has his mother's calm, ethical business temperament, as well as his grandmother Helen's social and optimistic spirit and love of performing. He will always remember his grandmother saying, "People here live better than the royalty in Europe." She wanted him always to be thankful for his many blessings.

Christine, my sister Sally's first daughter, born April 8, 1971, has her great-grandmother Karolina's determined spirit of faith and love. She has a degree in psychology and is a wife, mother, homemaker, and writer. She also loves technology, just like her grandmother Helen did.

"I remember playing 'dress up' in front of the child's vanity at Grandmother Helen's home," Christine recalls. She remembers the freedom her grandmother gave to her and to all the children. They were able to be themselves and "even listen to Christmas music when it wasn't Christmas!" She remembers when her grandmother tape-recorded the children singing and laughing and never discouraged them. Christine developed a love of drama and performing like her grandmother and performed in theater throughout her high school years. She told Grandma Helen, however, that she could not sing and was a member of the "singing impaired." With her usual optimistic faith, Helen's response was, "Nonsense! If you can talk, you can sing!"

2004
The Demetriades Family

Christine remembers her grandmother watching "TBN Church TV." She will never forget her kindness, strength, and willingness to give of herself. She is thankful for her generosity as she sent money to help with Christine's college tuition. Christine offered to pay her back when she came to visit in Phoenix, but her grandmother refused, saying, "Just clean the bathroom and wash my clothes and call it even!"

Christine's husband **Christopher** is currently a Marine Captain, making us all very proud with his service to our country including the recent liberation of Iraq. The family has recently moved to Okinawa for three years. Their children, **Peter Christopher**, born June 5, 1996, **Meagan Jo Anne**, born September 15, 1994, and Christine's daughter, **Emily Elizabeth**, born December 30, 1988, are members of Karolina's fifth generation.

Peter has his great-grandmother Helen's determination in being a good student. He loves a challenge and has a good sense of humor. Like Helen, Peter loves reading and learning, which inspire his quick wit.

Meagan already blesses us with her great-great-grandmother Karolina's loving and determined spirit. She quickly anticipates what needs to be done and pitches in to help her grandmother Sally. She is beautiful, artistic, and funny. She loves to be with family and has the cheerful, sparkling spirit of Karolina and Helen.

Emily has her great-grandmother Helen's spirit of self-confidence and her love of music and dancing. Like Helen, she has a beautiful singing voice, is an accomplished student, and loves reading and riding horses.

2001 The Farkas Family

Jenny, Sally's second daughter, born July 26, 1974, has her great-grandmother Karolina's love of God and family. She is one of my "sisters in the Lord." She encourages me and helps me when I need a "faith lift." I still have a beautiful Valentine's Day card she made for me with the love scripture of 1 Corinthians 13:8.

Besides being my prayer partner, Jenny is also a dedicated wife, mother, homemaker, singer, pianist, artist, writer, and gardener. She also loves to travel. Her Hungarian husband

Zoltan is a research instrument maker for Arizona State University's Physics and Astronomy Department. We are excited about his recent work on the Global Spectrometer and on the Mars Rover. My mother was so proud of him, technology lover that she was.

Jenny remembers her grandmother Helen's sense of humor and her love for hats—lots of hats! She remembers Helen tap-dancing on the tile floor wearing a large fur hat. Now Jenny's darling daughter **Maryanne Sarah,** born November 23, 1999, loves hats, too! As a baby Maryanne loved to wear just a big hat and a smile! Maryanne, a member of Karolina's fifth generation, loves music and sings and dances, like her great-grandmother Helen.

At my mother's funeral Maryanne pointed off to the side of the crowd and called out, "Grandma!" She must have seen her great-grandmother there, watching from eternity.

Jeremy, Sally's son, born August 9, 1980, has Karolina's determined spirit of love and faith. Like his grandmother Helen he supports recycling of our earth's natural resources and has an optimistic faith that "things will be OK." He has her love of music and is an accomplished drummer, performing for five years with his band, Atkins Lane.

Jeremy 2004

The musical influence of my mother and grandparents lives on in the family today. Several of the Grabiec children had operatic voices, and some could sing old country and coal-miner songs, word for word, even in their 80s! Other musical talent includes Nancy and Nick singing and playing the piano; John singing, directing, and playing hand bells; Sally and Jenny singing; Bob singing and playing the harmonica; Jeremy playing the drums; Liz playing the violin; and Zac dancing and, in his youth, singing with the Phoenix Boy's Choir.

A few of the other Grabiec family members who appreciate good music of all types include Audrey and her family singing and performing, and Carole Jane and her daughter Karyn, and son-in-law Bill Regitz, working in support of the Pennsylvania Academy of Music.

There are many other family stories waiting to be told. Each story is unique and may encompass the good and the bad, the humorous and the sad. As we allow Him, God will inspire us to share our faith, love, and the values of our heritage. I pray we don't neglect these most important issues of life.

Reflections

Since my youth, O God, you have taught me, and to this day I declare your marvelous deeds. Even when I am old and gray, do not forsake me, O God, till I declare your power <u>to the next generation</u>, your might to all who are to come. Psalm 71:17-18

No one is perfect, but the world is a better place because of my grandmother Karolina and my mother, Helen. Karolina came to America with nothing and yet laid the foundation for her descendants to have opportunities to not only succeed in career pursuits, but also to share their faith and love.

I am thankful for Karolina's life and sacrifice in holding on through tough times—working and surviving, yet all the while enjoying and loving her family. Karolina's spirit of determination, love, and faith lived on in her children. Their families brought happiness to each other and brought opportunities to share life and love. Karolina taught them the importance of family unity. She taught them how to forgive each other. Even as they grew up, married, and lived apart, they never separated emotionally or spiritually.

I am also blessed to have known and experienced the loving spirit of Karolina as it lived on in my mother, Helen. When I look at her family and her life, it's easy to understand why she was so happy—singing, dancing, teasing, laughing, and loving.

Mom had a forgiving attitude, was calm and thoughtful, had wit and humor, and was beautiful inside and out. I remember Mom's smile. I still sense her faith and her calm yet spirited enthusiasm. She was a treasure on earth to me and will always live in my heart and memory. Her spirit lives on in me. It lives in my sisters and brothers. I'm thankful for it. I pray that I can share that spirit with my children, grandchildren and great-grandchildren and that they, too, will be thankful.

I believe that all who share in the lives of Karolina's family will share in that spirit. I feel the flow of love between the past and the present. That flow can be stifled, or it can be shared. When I talk to Grandmother Karolina's children, my aunts and uncles, I feel the warmth and the mental energy to tell their story for future generations. Their lives and most of their children's lives have exemplified consistency and stability in their jobs, in their families, in their communities, and in other responsibilities of life.

Why did Karolina have such a great influence on my life? Why do I feel so close to her? She was so sweet, yet strict in a quiet sort of way. Her love for her children and grandchildren still inspires me today. Her kind but firm foundation of values has inspired me, not only in raising my two children, but also for thirty-eight years of teaching. I feel her love and want to share it with future generations so that the love of Grandmother Karolina and Helen are never forgotten.

Karolina and Helen trusted that God was in control of their lives. This is the Spirit that lives on in us today—His spirit! Their determination, love, and faith are now ours and came from Him! Only He can give us a new spirit with a loving heart—a heart of flesh and not of stone (Ezekiel 36:26). It is His love we share amongst ourselves and return to Him. This is the Spirit that lives on in us today.

The most important thing I can share with my son and daughter and to all of Karolina's descendants, now and in the future, is God's love. Nothing else matters if they don't experience that.

Karolina's spirit lives on in those who love!

*You are the light of the world.
Let your light shine before men, that they may see your good deeds
and praise your Father in heaven. Matthew 5:14a,16*

"Love Never Fails"

Love is patient, love is kind. It does not envy,
It does not boast, it is not proud.

It is not rude, it is not self-seeking,
It is not easily angered, it keeps no record of wrongs.

Love does not delight in evil
But rejoices with the truth.

It always protects, always trusts,
Always hopes, always perseveres.

Love never fails.

I Corinthians 13: 4-8a

Epilogue

Visiting Galloway, West Virginia, brought back memories of the past to my mother and her siblings. In 1963, Dad drove our family to Galloway. We picked up Mom's sisters Frances in Peoria, Illinois, and Betty in Bedford, Ohio. Mom wanted to find the house where she was born. She also wanted to see the old schoolhouse she had loved as a child. When she saw it, she remarked at how "small" it looked compared to how large it had seemed to her as a child. The school house was torn down ten years later in 1973-74.

Frances and Betty also wanted to see where they had played as children. Frances had tried years earlier to find her favorite "peanut doll," which she hid in the rafters of her home. But the houses had been torn down long ago.

Helen in Front of Birth Home in Galloway

However, she did enjoy visiting with her old Galloway friends, and seeing the school once more.

Dr. David Stokely Hays was the beloved horse-and-buggy coal-company doctor (and dentist) who treated the Grabiec family many times until they left Galloway in 1929. Right after they left, Dr. Hays treated many ill and dying residents during the typhoid fever outbreak in the fall of 1930. I believe it was a miracle that the Grabiec family had left just in time. Uncle Frank often wondered what had happened to Dr. Hays. In doing my research I found out that he worked in the area from 1913 until his death in 1939. Returning from a call in the early morning hours of April 21, 1939, Dr. Hays was killed by a train at the Fleming B & O train grade crossing. To prevent more such accidents, an overpass was built on January 20, 1941, over what is now Route 77.

Frank Jr. visited Galloway, West Virginia, several times after he left in 1929 as a boy of eight. He remembers visiting in 1980 with a former neighbor, Mrs. Honc, who ran the old "pool hall with the old fans in the ceiling." He quoted her as saying, "I'm operating a pool hall in Galloway now and have never played a game of pool!"

Underground slag fires in Galloway burned for years beginning in the 1950s, filling the air with smoke and drying up the beautiful green hills. The locals described to me the scene they remembered at night, with the "pretty blue and yellow glow of the burning slag piles." In contrast to their "beauty at night," however, the rain made the fumes stink up the air. The millions of gallons of trapped water also caused occasional blow-outs and landslides.

In 1984, after twelve years of planning, a land reclamation project began. The smoldering fires were flooded with water, causing so much billowing black stinking smoke that during those days the residents could not even see the sun. Today the slag piles (or gob piles as they were often called) burn no more. The five acres of slag piles and seventy acres of land over the old mines were graded and replaced with seventy-five acres of vegetation. The cost of the project was estimated to be $1.55 million. When the Grabiecs went back on occasional visits years later, they were glad to see that the burning had stopped and the grass on the hills was becoming green again.

The sulfur-filled creek with the "yellow water" where the Grabiec children remembered playing has also been cleaned up. Limestone was added which put phosphorous in the water and removed the sulfur. Once again fish are able to thrive in Simpson Creek. When it rains, however, more sulfur leaches out of the mines and the water yellows up again temporarily.

In March 2004 I journeyed back to Galloway with my cousin Carole Jane, her husband Fred, and their daughter Karyn who drove her motor home. In 1985 a new post office had been built on the main road, and it was there that we visited with many of the friendly town folk and found out who else to talk to and where they lived.[20]

2004 Anna Katula Paskey

"**Anna Paskey** is the best person to talk to," they told us. "She'll remember the Grabiecs when they lived here in Galloway." We found her in the nearby town of Philippi, residing at Mansfield Place. She told us that her General Store on the main road had closed in 1999. Now ninety, she loved having company and enjoyed telling us about her life and friends in Galloway.

Anna Paskey was one of Betty Grabiec's best friends in Galloway. The story of Anna's elopement at age sixteen is unforgettable, so I include it here.

> In 1930 Anna had rejected Joe, an admirer from Chicago, who wanted to marry her so desperately that he had her name tattooed on his arm! She had fallen in love with twenty-one-year-old Samuel Paskey from a neighboring town, and they decided to elope. For $5 she found a beautiful dress, size twenty. "I only weighed ninety-eight pounds at the time!" she laughs as she tells the story. "But I knew it had a lot of good material in it which I could use to make more clothes later."

Knowing her mother would never approve, Anna told her she was going to Clarksburg to find a job. She put on the size-twenty dress, tied a wide sash around her waist, gathering in all the material, and put on her dress shoes and angora tam. When Sam drove up in his Chevy Roadster, she ran out to greet him. He took one look at her, and his expression said it all!

"Don't say anything about my dress," she said, excitedly. "I think I look like a bride!" and off they went.

At the county seat Anna said she was seventeen, thinking that was old enough for a license. The clerk told Anna she was too young to get a marriage license. "I thought even a twelve-year-old could get married," she protested. She was told she could marry with her parents' permission. So, Sam was ready to take her home to speak to her parents. Anna knew her parents would never give their permission, so they drove fifty-five miles to the next town. Not taking any chances, she told the clerk she was twenty-one. They succeeded in getting their license and were married there.

For a wedding gift, Sam bought Anna a sewing machine which she later used to make many beautiful clothes. Anna's mother, however, did not speak to her for two years!

A war memorial stands across the street from the Post Office in Galloway. The Grabiecs have always been proud and patriotic Americans. Having lived through wars, they appreciate the freedoms that are paid for with the lives and sacrifices of many. Their immigrant mother, Karolina, taught them well that freedom is never "free."

As I hold Grandmother Karolina's immigration documents and Grandfather Frank's citizenship papers, I give thanks to God for their courageous sacrifices and for the freedoms we inherited. We need to teach our children about the price our parents and grandparents paid for our freedoms and teach them the patriotic songs of America, such as "America the Beautiful," "God Bless America," and others.

God gives us memory so we can appreciate *later* what we do not appreciate today. With my parents and grandparents gone now for many years, I still get inspiration from the remaining Grabiec family members. I also realize that our children are watching us. They will see how we respond to the call for dedication to preserving those freedoms.

I pray for a reawakening of godly character in each of us and a return to biblical values of integrity and honesty as was demonstrated in the lives of Karolina and Helen. Wisdom, discernment, strength, and love can all be attained by studying God's Word—His "love letters" to us here on earth. And then the spirit of love will continue to live on in future generations.

Karolina 1945

Appendix[21]

Brief History of Karvina, Czechoslovakia
and
The Daughter Left Behind

The town of Karvina has had a tumultuous history. In 1620 the people of Czechoslovakia lost their national independence to the Austro-Hungarian Empire at the Battle of White Mountain. For the next 300 years they were ruled by Austria. Thus, my maternal grandparents listed Austria as the place from which they emigrated, Frank in 1910 and Karolina 1913, even though their place of birth was Karvina, Czechoslovakia. The families they left behind, including Mañia, their first child, were left to deal with the rest of Czechoslovakian history.

Mañia was three when World War I began in Europe after the murder of the Austro-Hungarian Archduke Francis Ferdinand. In 1917 the United States entered to fight for democracy with the Allied Powers and twenty other nations. At the end of World War I in 1918, United States President Woodrow Wilson promoted the idea of the right to self-determination, and the Czechoslovakian Federation was formed out of two pieces of the former Austro-Hungarian Empire.

Twenty years later when Mañia was twenty-eight, France and the United Kingdom agreed in the Munich Agreement of 1938 to force the stable democracy of Czechoslovakia to cede to Germany. In 1939 when Hitler invaded Czechoslovakia and established a German "protectorate," she had to prove for five generations that she was not Jewish. In May 1945 parts of Czechoslovakia were liberated.

In 1948 when Mañia was thirty-eight, the communists took over. Stalin promised then United States President Roosevelt and British Prime Minister Churchill that there would be "free elections as soon as possible." He did not allow the elections, however, and Czechoslovakia remained a communist Soviet satellite country.

When Mañia was fifty-eight in 1968, Czechoslovakia's leader, Alexander Dubček, tried to inspire what was called "socialism with a human face" in an attempt to give the people more freedom of expression. Because of this, the Soviets invaded Czechoslovakia that year.

Twenty-one years later, in 1989 when Mañia was seventy-nine years old, communism collapsed across Eastern Europe. After the June elections the differences between the Czechs and Slovaks were awakened. On January 1, 1993, in a peaceful settlement, Czechoslovakia was split into two nations. Prague was to remain the capital of the Czech Republic, and Bratislava became the capital of Slovakia.

It is interesting to know some of the major events that happened in Karvina while my Aunt Mañia was living. A Christmas card sent to her in the year 2000 was returned marked "*Décédé.*" However, we do not know the exact date of her death. Most in our family got to visit with her only twice when she visited in America, but many of them are together now for eternity!

Notes

Chapter 1
1. We pronounce it Grā´ bek. Our Grandmother Karolina pronounced it Grä´ byetz. Alternate spellings included Grabieck and Crabec.
2. On his retirement application his birth date is listed as December 24. He may have forgotten his exact birth date due to several major head injuries, or it could have been transcribed incorrectly by the person filling out his application form for him.
3. *Webster's Encyclopedic Dictionary* (New York: Lexicon Publications, Inc., 1989), 720.
4. Ibid, 711.

Chapter 2
5. "North German Lloyd *Kaiser Wilhelm der Grosse*: The First Four-Stacker," 2001, available from www.LostLiners.com (29 June 2004).
6. The Jeff Newman Collection available from www.GreatShips.net.
7. "*Kaiser Wilhelm der Grosse,*" *Early 20th Century Ocean Liners,* 8 October 2002, available from www.LostLiners.com (29 June 2004).
8. Michael P. Palmer, *"Kaiser Wilhelm der Grosse," Palmer List of Merchant Vessels,* 16 March 2001, available from www.Geocities.com (29 June 2004).

Chapter 4
9. Fred Jones, Positive Classroom Management Conference, Fall 1998.

Chapter 6
10. Eventually, in 1966, eleven years after Karolina's death, Mañia was able to come to America to meet her brothers and sisters. In 1976 she returned with her husband Kleofas for her second and final visit to the United States.

Chapter 9
11. In her 1934 autograph book some of the interesting signatures include her best friend Stella Bozek; Walter Nemeth; Sophie Nemeth; a teacher, Ms. H. C. Flodin; Mildred Winestock; Frank Rossi who swallowed a goldfish and later manufactured accordions; her sisters Frances and Betty; her Franek cousins Mildred, Helen, and Henry's childish marks; and her mother Karolina's Polish words and signature.

Chapter 10
12. In 1955 when Karolina died, Verna locked herself in a room to be alone. For two weeks she only came out to eat. Her husband told the children she would be all right. She wrote the following poem after her broken heart began to have peace:

"My Mom"
I love thee Mom, my Mom. I love thee.
Though little was I when I learned of Him,
My first recognition of God was through thee,
A foresight of comfort restoring me.

Though our youth is now spent and time seems ceased,
No longer look I to see thy sweet face,
For our Lord has had His own good way;
But I understand.
I am filled with longing

Yet peace within my heart.
No more do I seek, "Where is My Mom?"
For thou sent thy death angel and lifted up my Mom.

Laid her to rest on Jesus our Savior's arm,
Softly, to the bosom of Jesus, my Mom,
Where she will know no more heartbreaking human pain.
Yet still little am I, oh Mom, my Mom.

Strengthened by faith in thee, in the God I love,
Who shall have His own way,
And call to me one day; and when I see the promise of thee
Mine eyes shall turn and I shall see thee again, my Mom.

My last memory of thee, dear Mom,
Thou didst plead to let thee be,
"For I am no king, but a child of God.
Though I love you my children and this lovely earth,
God has beckoned, 'Come home.'"

Then one by one, we bid farewell, our Mom.
We trust her to Jesus, till at
Jesus feet we'll meet again.
I thank our hallowed God, for Thy gift of knowing my Mom.

Thy lucid love is shining through forever, oh God.
Tenderly we love thee, Mom.
We loved thee then, we love thee now, and
We shall all love thee again in God's eternity.

In loving memory of Caroline* Grabiec by her children.
Verna Grabiec Kropp

*The spelling of Karolina's name became "Americanized" over the years.

176 / Watson

13. When it was time for the Berndt's to leave the family get-togethers, Uncle Otto always called out, "Get in the car, Ag!"

Chapter 11
14. December 16, 1944: "The Battle of the Bulge was a German counterattack in the Ardennes during the Second World War. Concentrating all his remaining reserves, Marshal von Rundstedt took advantage of foggy weather and a thinly held American front to break through and penetrate deep into Belgium, creating a bulge in the Allied lines. Antwerp, the main Allied supply base, was simultaneously bombed. A greatly outnumbered U. S. force held out heroically at Bastogne, until relieved by Allied forces which attacked the salient from the north and south, regained the initiative and resumed the offensive. The German advance was checked (January 1945) after it had penetrated fifty miles." (*The New Lexicon Webster's Encyclopedic Dictionary,* New York: Lexicon Publications, Inc.,1989, p. 128).
15. 1945 Family Reunion. Back: Elmer, Jim, Otto, Carl, Joe G., Joe K., Si. Seated: Ann, Helen holding Nancy, Agnes holding Earl, Betty holding Joey, Karolina holding Jimmie Lou, Verna holding Frannie, Frances, June. Front: Audrey Ann, Betty Jo, Richard, Carole Jane

Chapter 13
16. Some of Mother's good opera friends were Lucille Harney, Elizabeth Miller, Thea Dryfout, and Alice Mathis.
17. A few of the other operas and light operas in which she performed included the following:
>Johann Strauss' *Die Fledermaus*
>Giacomo Puccini's *La Bohèm* and, *Madama Butterfly*
>Sigmund Romberg's *Student Prince*, *Desert Song*, and *The New Moon*
>Franz Lehár's *The Merry Widow*
>Friml and Hooker's *The Vagabond King*
>Richard Rodgers and Oscar Hammerstein's *Oklahoma* and *Carousel*

Mom took us to some of her rehearsals. As the lead singer playing the part of "Bill" in *Carousel* sang "My Little Girl," he looked over at Nancy, Sally and me, little girls at the time, and sang it to us. We loved it!

18. After having lived with the Hopi for thirty years, Mr. Billingsley adopted a Hopi girl and was considered honorary Chief White Mungwee of the Hopi tribe at that time.

19. I can still remember them singing some of their favorites hymns which included the following:

>"In the Garden"
>"Beyond the Sunset"
>"Rock of Ages, Cleft For Me"
>"Some Day the Silver Chord Will Break"
>"My Faith Looks Up to Thee"
>"I Need Thee Every Hour"
>"Trust and Obey"
>"God Be With You 'til We Meet Again"
>"It is Well With my Soul"
>"The Old Rugged Cross"
>"Just a Closer Walk With Thee"
>"His Eye is on the Sparrow"
>"What a Friend We Have in Jesus"
>"Sweet Hour of Prayer"
>"Showers of Blessings"
>"Leaning on the Everlasting Arms"
>"Just as I Am"
>"My Jesus I Love Thee"

Epilogue

20. Some of the people we interviewed in March of 2003 while researching information in Galloway include:

    Anna Katula Paskey who shared stories of growing up with the Grabiecs in Galloway

Roger Mayle who took us on a tour of the old "Westside Shanty" area and gave us information about the location of Katie's murder

Geneva Phelps who wrote *We Were We Are: Fleming, West Virginia, District History Volumes I, II, and III*, and shared with me her video about local mining history

Hilda and Milton Bartlett who generously shared information they had and directed me to Geneva Phelp's research.

Others we visited with include Betty and Guido Cavallo, Shirley Hamrick, Kelly and Jeff Marshall, Icie and Joe Takacs, Myrtle Vucketich, Jim Wagner

Appendix

21. Information was compiled from family discussions, old news clippings in my mother's Bible, and from the following:

The Columbia Encyclopedia, 5th Edition, Columbia University Press, 1955.

"Czechs, Slovaks Ring in '93 in Separate Nations" and "A New Country, but What to Call it?" *The Arizona Republic*, January 1, 1993, Section A, p. 15.

ESL Focus on the Czech Republic, www.eslfocus.com/nationsfolder/foczech/foczech03.

The New Lexicon Webster's Encyclopedic Dictionary, New York: Lexicon Publications, Inc., 1989.

Acknowledgements

I am thankful to many for information and support in writing this true story.

—The patience and support of my husband, Jesse, who said "Go for it!" when I mentioned writing this family history

—My mother, Helen, and aunts and uncles who shared photos and stories of their lives in West Virginia, Illinois, and Arizona with me over the years

—My sister Nancy for her copyediting, photo editing, research, memories, and for her daily patience and encouragement

—My sister Sally and brothers Herb and John for their memories and encouragement

—My daughter Liz, my son Zac, and my nieces and nephews for their memories of their Grandmother Helen

—My cousins and friends for their photos and memories

—My cousin Carole Jane, her husband Fred, and their daughter Karyn for taking me to Galloway, West Virginia, to get first-hand information

—My new friends in Galloway

—My friend Nancy Hagener who told me about Tom Bird's writing class

—My teacher Tom Bird who taught me how to release my author within

—Peter Yurich for historical information and miners' photo of Grandpa Frank

—My book designer, Jamie Saloff, of Saloff Enterprises

—My book cover artist, Manjari Henderson, of Manjari Graphics

—My copy editor, Beth Phillips, of Eagle Eye Editor

—My God who inspired me through it all!

Index

A

Albright, Lois; 105, 107, 140
Alexander, Harriet; 146
Andrew, Dave; 122
Apache Trail; 89
Appalachian Mountains; 15
Aragon Ballroom; 62, 139
Arizona; 79, 111
    Apache Junction; 105
    Dewey; 111, 155
    Douglas; 113
    Goldfield; 89, 142
    Phoenix; 64, 69-71, 73, 80-91, 97, 104, 113, 123, 140, 141
        16th Street; 88
        E. Cocopah; 88
        E. Mohave; 82
        Glendale Avenue; 88
        Godfrey Street; 80
        Lincoln Drive; 88
        Solar Drive; 110
        South Central Avenue; 89
    Prescott; 66, 104, 150
    Scottsdale; 131
    Tempe; 89
    Tucson; 80, 143
Arizona State Electronics Association; 70
Arizona State University; 125, 158
Arrowhead Coal Company; 97
Atkins Lane; 159
Austria; 6, 11, 171

B

Bach Festival; 142
Baldwin Wallace College; 142
Bartlett Lake; 110
Battle of the Bulge; 84, 176
Battle of White Mountain; 171
Belgium; 176
Berndt, Agnes; 67, 68, 86, 89, 93, 133. See also Grabiec, Agnes
Berndt, Earl William; 67, 68
Berndt, Leslie Steven; 68
Berndt, Linda Susan; 2, 68
Berndt, Otto; 67, 68, 86, 89, 134, 176
Bielczyk, Kleofas; 72, 73, 76, 174
Bielczykova, Mañia; 72. See also, Grabiec, Mañia
Billingsley, M. W.; 105
Blue Bird Mine; 89, 142
Boice, Rev. Dr. William S. ; 104
Bristow, Mrs.; 91
Buchanan, Archie; 88
Buchanan, Hayden Lee; 88, 142
Buchanan, Jessie; 88, 142
Bud Brown's Barn; 112
Bulanda, Betty; 66, 67, 73, 76, 141, 165. See also Grabiec, Elizabeth (Betty)
Bulanda, Carl; 66, 67, 73, 76
Bulanda, James Edward; 67
Bulanda, Jean; 67
Bulanda, Joe; 66
Bulanda, Marilyn Elizabeth; 67, 141
Bulanda, Tillie; 66

B (Cont.)

Burr Elementary School; 59
Bushnell Hospital; 85

C

California; 88
    Van Nuys; 88
Camp Chorrera; 82
Canada; 156
Carnegie Hall; 107
Cernuska, Mary; 89
Cernuska, Mike; 61, 89
Certified Electronics Technician; 150
Chicago Civic Opera Company; 62
Chicago Theater; 140
Chicago Tribune; 53, 62
Christian Appalachian Project; 102, 135
Churchill, Winston; 172
coal mining; 6, 9, 15, 16, 31, 32, 96
    black lung; 17, 96
    company houses; 15
    company store; 16
    gob piles; 166
    mining accident of 1925; 33
    scabs; 33
    scrip, 16
    slag fires; 166
    unions; 32
Colorado; 88, 96
    La Junta; 96, 97
    Oak Creek; 96-100, 149
    Steamboat Springs; 98
Cowman, L. B.; 147
Crabec; 173
Crane Technical High School; 58
Czech Republic; See Czechoslovakia
    Prague; 172
Czechoslovakia; 5-7, 9, 13, 40, 72-77, 141, 151, 152, 156
    Karvina; 5-7, 9, 13, 74, 98, 171, 172
    map of; 5
    Oder River; 6
    Ostrava-Karvina; 6
    Stare Mesto Frestat; 5, 6
Czechoslovakian Federation; 171

D

Dairy Queen; 124
Davis, Adele; 127
Demetriades, Christine; 129. See also Nardozzi, Christine
Demetriades, Christopher; 158
Demetriades, Meagan Jo Anne; 158
Demetriades, Peter Christopher; 158
doughnuts; 122
Dubcěk, Alexander; 172
Dunn Coal Company; 97
Dyna Tronics; 70, 150

E

Eichenaur's Health Food Store; 127
Eklund, Elizabeth. See also Watson, Elizabeth Ann
Eklund, Eric; 156
Electronics Hall of Fame; 70
Ellis Island; 13
Encanto Park Band Shell; 104
Encanto Park Lagoon; 141

F

Family Life Radio KFLR; 146
Farkas, Jenny; 158, 159. See also Nardozzi, Jenny
Farkas, Maryanne Sarah; 159
Farkas, Zoltan; 158
Ferdinand, Archduke Francis; 171
Field Museum; 53
First Christian Church; 104
43rd Tank Battalion; 84
France; 84, 85, 145, 171
    Nancy; 84
Franek, Agnes; 14
Franek, Joseph; 5, 9, 18, 47
Franek, Karolina; See Grabiec, Karolina
Franek, Mary Marcal; 5, 10, 40, 47, 98, 156
Franek, Rudolph; 6, 10, 11, 14, 46, 51, 62, 152

G

Galloway School; 35
    school bell; 37
German '88'; 84
Germany; 11, 12, 145, 171
    Bremen; 12
    Bremerhaven; 12
Gewelke, Annie; 71, 72, 76, 89, 96, 97, 122. See also Grabiec, Annie
Gewelke, Cynthia Joy; 72
Gewelke, Donald Barry; 72
Gewelke, Douglas Steven; 72
Gewelke, Elmer; 72
Gewelke, Laura Jean; 72
Global Spectrometer; 159
golabki; 65, 95
Grabiec, Agnes; 14, 21-25, 27-34, 36-40, 44, 49-56, 57-62, 67, 82. See also Berndt, Agnes
Grabiec, Annie; 19, 29-34, 38, 49, 71, 79, 82. See also Gewelke, Annie
Grabiec, Carolyn Lee; 69, 142
Grabiec, Denise Lavonne; 71
Grabiec, Diana Kay; 71
Grabiec, Elizabeth (Betty); 13, 19, 27, 32, 35, 39, 46, 57, 60, 66, 167. See also Bulanda, Betty
Grabiec, Frances; 13-14, 15-19, 27-34, 35-40, 43-47, 57, 65. See also Meardy, Frances
    Morgantown rescue; 43
Grabiec, Frank Jr.; 18, 19, 27-34, 36-40, 42-47, 49-56, 57-62, 65-77, 80, 97, 112, 166
    ax murder; 42
    bell tower; 66, 69
Grabiec, Frank Sr.; 6, 9-14, 19, 96, 142, 149, 171
    arrested; 38
    born; 6, 173
    Certificate of Naturalization; 96
    died; 99
    emotional breakdown; 37
    married; 13
    mining accident; 33
    truck crash; 98
Grabiec, Gary Steven; 69
Grabiec, Helen; 17, 30-34, 46, 133-138. See also Hayden, Helen
    Associate of Arts Degrees; 109
    baptized; 103
    beautician; 58
    born; 17
    breakdown; 128
    cataracts; 129
    classical music; 21
    coal-miners' union song; 32
    congestive heart; 134
    diabetes; 134
    died; 137
    divorced; 131
    Frank Sr. & Helen reunited; 97
    hair; 135
    high blood pressure; 134
    high cholesterol; 134
    high school graduation; 60
    Holy Communion; 58
    James and Helen meet; 80
    married; 81
    parenting; 115-131
    Phoenix, moves to; 79
    poppy seeds, grinding; 123
    prejudice, overcoming; 105
    remarried; 130
    starts school; 36
    swim team; 59
    voice lessons; 62
    war effort; 83
Grabiec, Joseph; 6
Grabiec, Joseph David; 18-19, 24, 29, 36, 53, 57-62, 70, 71, 82, 84, 89, 95-100, 134
Grabiec, June; 69. See also Keck, June
Grabiec, Karolina
    America, arrives in; 13
    asthma; 79, 95
    bakery, working in a; 50
    baptized; 91
    bootlegging; 44, 45
    born; 5
    Chicago, arrives in; 13
    Chicago, returns to; 46
    christening of Agnes; 14
    christening of Mañia; 10
    christening of Verna and Frances; 13
    died; 98, 99
    Karolina & Frank meet; 9
    Mañia visits gravesite; 75
    married; 13
    Phoenix, moves to; 79
    pneumonia; 64
    Pullman car, cleaning; 50
    West Virginia, moves to; 15
Grabiec, Kathleen Joyce; 71
Grabiec, Mañia; 9-14, 17, 40, 72-77, 171-172, 174. See also Bielczykova, Mañia.
Grabiec, Marlene Susan; 70, 142

G (Cont.)

Grabiec, Matreena; 70, 71, 89, 95
Grabiec, Veronica (Verna); 13, 14, 25, 34, 35, 36, 44, 46, 57, 63. See also Kropp, Verna
Grabiec, Wayne Carl; 69
Grabieck; 173
Grand Canyon; 76
Great Depression; 50, 55, 123, 127
Grobowski, Joe; 42
Guadalcanal; 69
Guam; 86

H

Hageman's Garage; 98
Hawaii; 152
Hayden, Bertha; 88, 92
    harmonica; 92
Hayden, Bonnie; 88
Hayden, Dixie; 88
Hayden, Helen. See also Grabiec, Helen
Hayden, Herbert E. (Jim's father); 81, 88
Hayden, Herbert Thomas; 107-114, 120, 150
Hayden, James Alfred; 69, 71, 80, 83, 84, 108-114, 115, 121-131, 135, 139-143, 152, 165
    died; 112
    Mail Carrier, U. S. Postal Service; 87
    retired; 109
    wounded; 84
Hayden, Jimmie Lou; 84, 116-131, 135, 142. See also Watson, Jimmie Lou
    All State High School Chorus; 125
    baptized; 103
    born; 84
    Miss Polonia; 146
    YMCA Youth Chorus; 145
Hayden, John W. (James' brother); 88
Hayden, John Robert; 74, 89, 107, 113, 116, 117, 122, 134, 137, 150-154, 159
    vision of parents; 152
Hayden, Judy; 88
Hayden, Madge; 81. See also Mitchell, Madge
Hayden, Nancy Lee; 28, 83-90, 94, 108, 111, 116, 121-131, 134, 147, 148, 155-160
Hayden, Sally Sue; 88, 95, 138, 148, 157. See also Nardozzi, Sally
Hays, Dr. David Stokely; 18, 27, 28, 38, 166
head tax; 12
health; 79, 89, 96, 109, 120, 127, 131, 134, 135

Hitler, Adolph; 171
Hole-in-the-Rock Mountain; 89
homemaking; 120-125
Honc, Mrs.; 166
Hopitu; 105
Horseshoe Lake; 110
Hospice of the Valley; 136
Hungary; 150

I

Illinois
    Bartonville; 66, 141
    Chicago; 13-14, 45-47, 49-56, 57-62, 63-77, 79, 82-90, 97, 111, 139, 140
        12th Street; 53
        Chicago Avenue; 53
        Division Street; 62
        Huron Street; 53
        Lake Shore; 53
        May Street; 52
        Meade Avenue; 51, 72
        Milwaukee; 53
        North Bell Avenue; 55
        West Division Street; 51
        West Huron Street; 52
        Wicker Park Avenue; 55, 61, 80, 82
    Green Valley; 66
    Peoria; 66
        Fayette Street; 85
International Society of Certified Electronic Technicians; 70

J

Japan; 158
    Okinawa; 158
Jitney; 15, 17, 32

K

Kaiser Wilhelm der Grosse; 12
kapusta; 95
Katula, Anna; 39. See also Paskey, Anna
Katula, Mrs.; 23, 39
Keck, June; 55. See also Grabiec, June
kielbasa; 95
Kirkbride, Ann; 96
Kirkbride, Frances; 6, 96, 97

K (Cont.)

Kodak Brownie camera; 1
kolaczki; 24, 33, 95
koron; 12
Kropp, Audrey Ann; 25, 62, 64, 82, 83, 139, 140, 159
Kropp, Betty Jo; 64
Kropp, Frances Laura; 64
Kropp, Joseph; 63
Kropp, Joseph (son); 64, 87, 176
Kropp, Verna; 63, 64, 73, 83, 86, 98, 99, 139, 140, 174. See also Grabiec, Veronica (Verna)
    poem, "My Mom"; 174
Kusick, Rudy; 42

L

Lake Michigan; 53, 62
Leigh and Nardozzi Caterers; 149
Lewis, C. S.; 114
Lichner, Al; 45, 50, 58
Lichner, Ann; 6, 13, 45, 51, 58, 117
Lichner, Paul; 49, 51
Liszt, Franz; 7
Louisiana; 81

M

Mackinaw River; 66
mangle; 124
Mansfield Place; 167
Maricopa Technical College; 109
Mars Rover; 159
McLaughlin, Mignon; 111
Meardy, Carole Jane; 23, 62, 65, 85, 88, 140, 159, 167. See also Spencer, Carole Jane
Meardy, Frances; 65-77, 84, 85, 97, 110, 128, 140, 141, 165. See also Grabiec, Frances
Meardy, Gary; 141
Meardy, Richard Eugene; 65, 85, 86, 141
Meardy, Silas; 65, 66
Merry Makers; 112
Mexico; 156
Mitchell, Gus; 88
Mitchell, Madge; 88
Moffat Coal Company; 97
Morini, Rosalinda; 62, 80
Munich Agreement of 1938; 171

N

Nardozzi, Bob; 149, 159
Nardozzi, Carolyn; 138
Nardozzi, Christine; 149, 157. See also Demetriades, Christine
    Emily Elizabeth; 158
Nardozzi, Jenny; 149, 152, 158. See also Farkas, Jenny
Nardozzi, Jeremy; 149, 159
Nardozzi, Sally; 158, 159. See also Hayden, Sally Sue
Nebraska; 88
    Lincoln; 88
Nemeth, Julius; 13, 53, 61
Nemeth, William (Willie); 53, 61, 62, 79, 90, 141
Nevada; 76
    Las Vegas; 76
New Mexico; 113
    Albuquerque; 113
New York; 12, 107
    New York City; 13, 73

O

Ohio; 66, 142
    Bedford; 67, 165
        Alexander Road; 142
    Cleveland; 66
Oklahoma; 80, 81, 92
    Chickasha; 81, 88, 142
    Pauls Valley; 80

P

Paderewski, Ignace; 7
Painted Desert; 110
Panama Canal; 82
Papago Park; 90
parenting; 116-120, 130-131
Paskey, Anna; 167, 178. See also Katula, Anna
    elopement; 167
Paskey, Samuel; 167
Pearl Harbor; 82, 83
Pennsylvania Academy of Music; 160
Peterson, Rev. D. M. ; 91, 103
Petrified Forest; 110
Phoenix; 157
Phoenix Boy's Choir; 159

P (Cont.)

Phoenix Opera Company; 104
Phoenix Symphonic Choir; 104
Piaza, Joseph; 38, 42
Piaza, Katie; 42
Piercy, Rev. Jim; 104
pierogi; 63, 95
pierzyna; 6, 39, 141
Piestewa Peak; 88, 110, 141. See also Squaw Peak
Piwo; 99
Pokrzywa, Chester; 61
Poland; 11
Polish; 5, 6, 7, 17, 36, 39, 51, 56, 61, 64, 93, 94, 95, 99, 116, 122, 123, 140, 146, 174
polisinki; 95
Popovitch, Mr.; 45, 46
Porter, Cole; 104
posipka; 33, 123
Postal Telegraph; 58-59
Prince, Bob; 88
Prince, Elsie; 88
Prohibition; 44

Q

Quade, Nick; 109, 147, 156, 159

R

Reader's Digest; 111
recycling; 70, 127, 159
Regitz, Bill; 160
Regitz, Karyn; 76, 160, 167
Riverside Pool; 89
Roosevelt, Franklin D.; 32, 57, 83, 172
Rossi, Frank; 58
Route 66; 80

S

San Carlos Hotel; 80
school. See also Galloway School
    Catholic; 52, 58
    continuation; 58
scrip; 16
September 11, 2001; 136
Shedd Aquarium; 53
Simpson Creek; 167
Simpson Creek Collieries Company; 15, 16, 97
Slovakia; 172
    Bratislava; 172
Smith, Hannah Whitall; 114
South Korea; 113, 156
South Mountain; 141
South Mountain Park; 89
Soviets; 172
Spain; 156
Spencer, Carole Jane. See also Meardy, Carole Jane
Spencer, Fred; 140, 167
Squaw Peak; 88, 141. See also Piestewa Peak
St. John's Catholic Church; 14, 58
Stalin, Joseph; 172
Stevenson Park Church of Christ; 91, 103
Stump, Dr.; 96
Superstition Mountains; 142

T

Talcott School; 59
TBN Television Network; 127
Texas; 81, 88
    Camp Barkeley; 81
    Dallas; 88
    Ft. Worth; 88
Titanic; 10, 11, 12
Tovrea, Mr.; 80

U

U. S. Armed Forces; 145
U. S. Army; 61, 68, 81, 145, 150
U. S. Department of Defense; 113, 156
U. S. Navy; 68
Union League Boys Club; 54, 69
United Christian Youth Camp; 104
United Kingdom; 171
United States Marine Corps; 69
University of Phoenix; 131
Utah; 85
    Brigham City; 85

V

values; 34, 115, 139, 160, 162, 169
Verdi, Guiseppe; 104
Virginia; 149
    Gloucester Point; 149

W

Watson, Elizabeth Anne; 113, 145, 155, 159.
    See also Eklund, Elizabeth
Watson, Jesse; 134, 145
Watson, Jimmie Lou. See also; Hayden, Jimmie
    Lou
Watson, Zachary Andrew; 66, 145, 156, 159
Weldon Stables; 89, 141
Wells High School; 58
Wesson, Mrs.; 91, 92
Wesson, Nora; 92
West Virginia; 30, 32, 34, 41, 66, 91, 135
    Barbour County; 17
    Bluefield; 43
    Clarksburg; 32, 167
    Fairmont; 32
    Flemington; 15
    Galloway; 15-19, 22-50, 66, 68, 97, 140,
        165-169. See also; ax murder; 41
    Morgantown; 43
    Philippi; 167
    Simpson Creek; 32, 39, 40
        flood; 40
    Weston; 38, 96
White Castle; 53
white house on the hill; 38, 43
Wilson, Olivia; 98, 99
Wilson, Woodrow; 171
Winestock, Dr.; 63
Wisconsin; 54
    Salem; 54
Works Progress Administration (WPA); 57
World War I; 11, 12, 15, 171
World War II; 61-69, 82-86, 123, 127, 134
World's Fair, 1933-34; 53
Wrasena, Josaphine; 6

Y

YMCA; 69
YMCA Chauncy Ranch Camp; 69
YMCA Sky-Y Camp; 66
YMCA Youth Chorus; 145
Yurich, Peter; 149

Photo Index

Agnes' Christening Day, 14
Ann, Helen, Agnes, Betty, Frances, and Verna; 60
Anna Katula Paskey; 167
Annie and Elmer Gewelke; 72
Baby Helen; 18
Betty and Carl Bulanda; 67
Chicago Family Reunion; 86
Dad Holding Me in Utah; 85
Demetriades Family, The; 157
Farkas Family, The; 158
First Holy Communion; 58
First Miss Polonia in Phoenix; 146
Frank Jr. with Landlord; 61
Frank Sr. on Graveyard Shift; 96
Frank Sr. with Helen; 98
Frank Sr. with Karolina; 97
Galloway Road; 29
Galloway School; 35
Garden, The; 22
Grabiec Family, 1923; 18
Grabiec Family, 1929; 51
Grandma Karolina and Me with Her Dolls; 93
Grandma Karolina's Driveway; 99
Grandmothers Hayden and Grabiec; 93
Haunting Memories; 41
Hayden Family, The; 118

Helen in High School; 59
Helen and Jim; 82, 83
Helen and Opera Friends; 107
Helen in Front of Birth Home in Galloway; 165
Helen Walking in Phoenix; 101
Helen with Frank Rossi; 58
Helen's Girls Hanging Laundry; 124
Helen, Then and Now!; 153
Hilltop View of Galloway, West Virginia; 16
Hopitu Program; 106
Horse Posing with Mom in Arizona; 90
James and a Friend in the U. S. Army; 80
Jeremy, 2004; 159
Joseph and Matreena Grabiec; 71
Joseph as Postal Messenger; 59
Joseph, Karolina, and Frank Jr.; 60
June and Frank Grabiec Jr.; 69
Kaiser Wilhelm der Grosse; 13
Karolina, 4
Karolina 1945; 169
Karolina and Helen in Chicago; 79
Karolina with Helen's Girls; 92
Karolina with Her First Nine Grandchildren; 87
Karolina, James, and Helen, May 18, 1941; 81
Karvina, Czechoslovakia, 5
Kids in Grandma's Tubs 1948; 92
Kleofas' and Mañia's Wedding Photo; 72

Little Hayden Sisters; 103
Liz and Eric Eklund; 156
Mañia and Kleofas Bielczyk; 73
Mañia Meets Her Sisters and Brothers; 74
Mañia with her Grandparents Mary Marcal and
Joseph Franek; 47
Mañia's Christening Day; 10
Meardy Family, The; 65
My Favorite Doll; 93
Nancy and Nick; 148
Nardozzi Family, The; 149
New Neighborhood for the Grabiec Children; 49
Otto and Agnes Berndt; 68
Phoenix Symphonic Choir
Together at Karolina's Gravesite; 75
Verna and Joe Kropp; 64
Visit to Blue Bird Mine; 142
Watson Family, The; 145
Young Betty; 24
Young Frances; 24
Young Helen; 54

www.ingramcontent.com/pod-product-compliance
Lightning Source LLC
Chambersburg PA
CBHW071706090426
42738CB00009B/1688